This book is a masterpiece of contempora~~~~ ~~~~~~~~ ~~~ ~~~
Generational Leadership enables parents, teachers and pastors to join in a circle of respect, love, protection and development, to shape the next generations.

This is a ministry manual that every pastor needs to develop his team. It is a tool that every Christian teacher needs to be effective in his academic work, and a pearl for parents who are unwilling to let their children's childhood and adolescence pass without being intentional in discipling them.

With great optimism, the information on these pages will help us face the great challenges of our time, as well as the useless paradigms that are still prevalent in some circles to this day. Sometimes echoing great men of science, theologians, social reformers and artists, Dr. Leys reconciles us with such knowledge by offering us amazingly practical advice that will make reading this jewel one of the most enriching and valuable experiences we can have.

Hector Hermosillo
Founding pastor of Semilla de Mostaza, Mexico, Texas, California

Anyone who wants to have a church that's vibrant, full of life, and filled with young people, teenagers and children should read this book. It must be a priority for pastors today.

How many times have I heard pastors in Latin America wonder why there are no young people in their church? Or confess that their children love God, but not the church . . . If you really want a church that reaches the new generations you should read this book, but I give you a warning: if you are not willing to change, you better not read it, because in each chapter its author proposes changes.

I believe that God has something new in mind, and I think it has a lot to do with what my friend Lucas Leys wrote in this book.

Robert Barriger
Founding pastor of Camino de Vida, Peru

This book by Dr. Lucas Leys could not be more timely and necessary. World-wide, we are witnessing a rise of renewed interest in children and youth, especially when it comes to their education and human promotion. Even the United Nations' Organization for Global Education is calling for a great effort in support of the civil rights of children and adolescents across the globe. The church cannot lag behind, much less turn a deaf ear to such a need.

Today there are 260 million children who no longer go to school and 400 million others who will interrupt their education at some point and will never return to finish it. There are 800 million children (half of those in the world) who will leave school without the qualifications they need to work, mostly due to poverty. What will Christians do about this? How can we train with Christian values the generation of 6-25 –year olds– that today is under our responsibility? How will we make these people know that they are maturing in God's love, as it was manifested in Christ? These are the questions that Leys sets out to answer in these pages, emphasizing the formation of the Christian leaders who will undertake this task. Reading this book is indispensable for today's leaders and a must for the immediate future.

Dr. Pablo A. Deiros
President of International Baptist Seminary, Buenos Aires, Argentina

In every generation God raises up trailblazers to give us groundbreaking leadership with innovative wisdom. Lucas Leys is one of those leaders for this generation. In *Generational Leadership*, I believe he is clearly presenting the most effective plan for the church to reach out to this generation. This should be mandatory reading for every pastor and those working with children, students and families. I appreciate that this book is both well researched and incredibly practical. I know Lucas well. He is a man of integrity, brilliant, passionate and clearly is making a difference in the way we must look at how to do church.

Jim Burns, PhD.
Author; President of HomeWord

This book proposes the type of change that fills me with hope. Change and innovation should be constant in the church, since we have to continually renew ourselves in order to continue reaching the next generations. In this book Lucas provides a deep analysis of reality and proposes a consistent strategy to generate those changes that we always need.

I believe that the application of the leadership concepts detailed in this book has the potential of taking our new generation's ministries to a higher level of commitment to the life God dreamed for his church.

Chris Mendez
Pastor of Hillsong Buenos Aires, San Paulo and Monterrey

This book is simply brilliant. In its pages Dr. Lucas Leys, true to his direct, profound and practical style, leads us on a thoughtful and conscientious journey to review our way of building the church and the paradigms of working with the new generations. This handbook brings to pastors interested in church growth and to educators in general a fresh and updated proposal that will help focus the church's attention on the changes that we need. The content is accurate, relevant and urgent for today's church. Thank you, Lucas, for this new help manual for those of us who believe in working with the new generations!

Karen Lacota
Principal of Faith Christian School in Asunción, Paraguay; Author

The DeVos Urban Leadership Initiative has been partnering with Lucas Leys and e625 to bring *Liderazgo Generacional* through one-day training events to Spanish-speaking pastors here in the U.S. So, what a wonderful opportunity now to share *Generational Leadership* with the English-speaking world. The practical way that Lucas combines the neuroscience of the developmental stages of life with the mission of the church to make disciples makes this a book that every pastor and youth leader should read and reference. It is no longer enough to just say that the youth hold our future. We need to invest our time and our resources in our children and youth, developing them as disciples of Jesus. We need them to lead the church today and make it relevant for generations to come.

Eileen Kooreman, PhD
Director of DeVos Urban Leadership Initiative

Generational Leadership is a unique resource, extremely useful for pastors. From now on it should be a must read, especially for those who spend their lives forming the opinions and forging the character of the new generations, and who are aware of the urgent need to understand our times. Changes are happening at a speed that most of us never could have imagined, and no matter who we are or what we do, we can all make use of tools that help us expand our ministerial lungs instead of becoming victims of the passage of time. *Generational Leadership* is an invitation to understand the different areas of development and learning styles in human growth. Dr. Lucas Leys reveals in this book the secrets of how to think, act and respond positively to the paradigm changes that we urgently need.

Rev. Hermes Espino Q.
Pastor of Casa de Oración Cristiana, Panama

It is one thing to repeat knowledge and another to create it and this is what Dr. Lucas Leys does in this extraordinary research that proposes ideas with tangible transformative potential. In this book, Lucas explores with depth and grace a totally innovative proposal that he calls generational leadership. He identifies paradigms that we must overcome and then makes practical recommendations that we must urgently take into consideration. Possibly, one of the greatest virtues of the work is in the sincere and critical dialogue between the current ministerial realities and the paths that we must explore to reach the future in the ministries for the new generations.

This is a necessary reading, not only for pastors, and for leaders who want to effectively serve the new generations, but for fathers and mothers who want to better understand and contribute positively to the important processes of formation of their sons and daughters.

Dr. Samuel Pagán
Author and Dean of the Biblical Studies Center in Jerusalem

With his book *Generational Leadership* Lucas Leys presents key questions that each pastor needs to answer if he is interested not only in reaching new generations, but also in retaining the generations already present in his congregation. The content demonstrates years of scientific studies and academic research and also a passion to see the church grow and reach and retain each age group by making discipleship more effective.

This book will challenge you to question and examine what we have been doing, and will encourage you to improve strategies in order to continue advancing the kingdom of God during our times.

Tim Holland
Senior Pastor of Life Church-Mundo de Fe

This is an excellent and urgent contribution to the challenges posed by leadership relevant to the 21st century. Lucas Leys invites us in this text, with the passion that characterizes him, to build ministries that revolve around dialogue and connection, so that our service can have a clear eternal projection. I highly recommend it to every leader and pastor who longs to see his local church grow.

Dr. Christopher Shaw
CEO of Desarrollo Cristiano Internacional

Refreshing, challenging and revealing. That is what this book is. As I walked along these pages, I could not help feeling my heart fill with hope as I imagined the future of the Church of Christ in the Spanish-speaking world. Maybe it's the pastor's son in me. Perhaps it's the pastoral heart in me. It may be that as a father of teenagers I hope that today's church will provide a relevant purpose that will serve as a bridge between the church and future generations.

Full of biblical wisdom and clear arguments, Lucas invites us in this manual to broaden our vision of the future to accomplish the work of generational leadership, as we watch the Spirit challenge us to undertake the mission of being an influential church in the present time, with the ability of becoming transcendental to future generations.

Thank you, Lucas, for inviting us to rethink our methods without losing our compass.

Jacobo Ramos
Pastor of Global Ministry, Gateway Church

Lucas Leys is one of the most inspiring leaders I know. He is a prophetic voice to the global church that is trying to find its way forward in the midst of a rapidly changing world. In this much needed book, *Generational Leadership*, Lucas reminds us of God's heart for the family, the church, the next generation and how they all work together to make disciples and create the future. With both passion and clarity Lucas doesn't just tell us the "what," he gives us the "why" and "how" to advance God's kingdom in today's generation. Rarely do you come across a book with such compelling theology, vision, and strategy all woven together. I am both challenged and encouraged by this book and I believe you will be too. It's time to reach and raise up the next generation!

John Stickl
Lead Pastor of Valley Creek Church, North Texas

What this book proposes is literally "revolutionary" and, if it's read with the right spirit, I have no doubt that it will unleash a wave of mental and practical changes in thousands of pastors and leaders in Latin America. In fact, what he proposes is so solid and innovative that I anticipate that it will cause a wave of changes in the worldwide church.

I have known the author for many years and he never ceases to amaze me.

When I think that his innovation has reached its maximum expression, he surprises me again. His ministry has been more influential than we can know, because not only has it impacted the lives of thousands of attendees at his events and thousands of readers of his books, but it has also transformed the minds of many opinion leaders who literally changed their culture through conversations with Lucas in the intimate times backstage at his events.

In some circles Lucas is known as an eloquent preacher and someone who has the ability to be a "showman," but I don't know any showman who has the ability to also become a scientist who can go so deep in elucidating the needed strategies of the church, and this book is yet additional proof of that.

Lucas is a great innovator who always travels at a thousand miles per hour looking for "something else" and yet he has excellent interaction with people, and especially with his work team, which is probably the most competent I know.

Thank you, brother, for the time you've spent investigating this issue even in the midst of many trips, conferences, forums, retreats and crowds who listen to you. It's a great thing that you're Latin American.

Esteban R. Fernández
AED President Latin America, International Bible Society

GENERATIONAL LEADERSHIP

LUCAS LEYS

e625.com

GENERATIONAL LEADERSHIP

e625 - 2020

Dallas, Texas

e625 ©2020 by **Lucas Leys**

Originally published in Spanish under the title:

Liderazgo Generacional
Copyright © 2017 Lucas Leys

All Scripture quotations, unless otherwise indicated, are taken from the Holy Bible, New International Reader's Version®. NIrV®. Copyright © 1995, 1996, 1998 by Biblica Inc®. Used by permission. All rights reserved worldwide.

Translation by **David Ortíz**
Proofreading by **Lori Alberda**
Design by **JuanShimabukuroDesign @juanshima**

ALL RIGHTS RESERVED

ISBN: 978-1-946707-55-0

*To the pastors who get down on their knees
to ask God for the growth of the church.*

ACKNOWLEDGMENTS

Each book is the result of the work of more than one person, and in this particular one there are many people who contributed, consciously or not, in order for these pages to be written. God's grace is always the great source of all that I can do. Without his grace I cannot do anything, and that is why I begin by thanking my Lord for allowing me to work on this project.

Thanks to Valeria, Sophie and Max for supporting Dad as much as you do. Your lives teach me and inspire me.

Thank you Juan Shima for your work on this project, and above all for your friendship. It is a luxury to have someone by my side who understands teamwork as well as you do.

Many thanks to all the members of the amazing e625.com family. It is an undeserved honor to work with all of you.

CONTENTS

PASTORAL INTRODUCTION

There is something that has always intrigued me about Lucas Leys, and it's to see him always spreading two things: enthusiasm and peace. Lucas is a visionary entrepreneur, and like all of his kind, he is full of enthusiasm. What fills them with passion and enthusiasm is to be able to burst with something new, develop it, manage it and spread it. But often that adrenaline-filled enthusiasm of the entrepreneurs has a flip side. They often find themselves emotionally overwhelmed, unadjusted in their family life, financially unbalanced, and even spiritually unbalanced. Although they project an overflowing security on the surface, their inner self is filled with more uncertainties than certitude. But the interesting thing about Lucas is that he is filled with enthusiasm, while also living in peace, a trait seen more in the settler than in the pioneer. In other words, the leadership that works with the known and predictable.

By reading *Generational Leadership*, I can understand better why you can combine both characteristics. Lucas not only sees the needs of the church, which fills him with enthusiasm, but he has the peaceful demeanor of someone who has a perfectly developed plan for the church to meet those needs.

Indeed, the Church needs a new understanding and a new practice of discipleship. The Church has lived through wonderful spiritual experiences and growth. But it lacks the comprehensive living discipleship that affects all generations with relevant pastoring.

While reading *Generational Leadership*, the phrase "Lucas is a pontiff" came to mind again and again (I hope he doesn't change the way he dresses). The word "pontiff" means "bridge builder." The distance between where we are today as a church and where we should be is reached by a bridge called a plan. And Lucas not only knows where we should go, but proposes how to get there.

Generational Leadership is an architecture of discipleship that unites realities hitherto disintegrated. It is a bridge between "Sunday's best" and everyday life that enables the church-made disciples to influence all of our nations in a transformational manner, so that the disciples that the church is making affect the whole reality in our nations in a transformational way. It is a bridge between church and society, developing a cultural intelligence that allows God's people to be real without falling into a value trap.

Whoever reads this book carefully will notice that *Generational Leadership* is a bridge based on discipleship that unites the family and the church in order to obtain comprehensive and effective results. It connects the different stages of a person's life (childhood, preadolescence, adolescence, youth) to enable Christian discipleship to become effective in every moment and for every existential need.

The ancient pontiff used to have among his tasks the role of organizing the calendar and celebrating the holidays. Lucas offers in these pages extraordinary assistance in organizing the "generational discipleship calendar" for the lives of those whom God brings to us. With these ideas we will reduce the number of children we lose along the way and in each transition, while multiplying our opportunities to continue to extend the power of our local churches.

Generational Leadership builds a bridge that takes us from where we are now to where we should be going. Surely this is not a task for a single man or a single ministry, but one that's assigned to the whole church in our continent. I have no doubt that Lucas and e625, with *Generational Leadership*, are making an amazingly significant contribution that will mark a before and after in discipleship for the new generations.

Once again, the pontiff Lucas is a step ahead of us, showing us the way with great enthusiasm and without losing his peace.

Carlos Mraida
President of the council of pastors of the city of Buenos Aires, Argentina

DECLARATION OF INTENT

We all want to be more effective in influencing the new generations. The problem is not our intentions. I've yet to find a single pastor or leader, let alone a Christian mother, who does not believe that the spiritual formation of the new generations is important. *But why do so many children who at some point passed through a Christian church no longer congregate? Why do so many kids of good Christians decide to turn their back on their family's faith? Why do so many teenagers who participate in our meetings and get excited about the songs then choose to make decisions that are the opposite of what we preach? Why aren't there more and more university students coming to our congregations, if we are the salt of the earth, the light in the darkness, and the bearers of the true secret to an abundant life?*

Obviously, good intentions are not enough for a church and a family to develop disciples of Christ effectively. We need the eternal wisdom, a pinch of science, an accurate commitment and a romance with change. Yes, we already know the saying: Even though the gospel does not change, the way of sharing it must always be updated.

Those who work with the new generations are spies. They have secret information regarding the future of our societies, and protect confidential documents vital to the development or failure of their countries.

They may not be at the top of the salary scale, or of the popularity ranking in our cities, but they are the engineers of progress.

Those who invest their lives in forming the opinions and forging the character of the new generations are spies in tomorrow's land, craftsmen of the future, and architects of change. That is why I love spending time with them, and why I am passionate about helping them.

I believe in the church because I believe in God's plan, and I believe in the message we bring. What I don't believe is that we must stagnate where we are. We have to reach more children, adolescents and youth with the gospel of Jesus, and we must reduce the number of children we lose along the way. I refuse to think of churches that are declining, of congregations that are aging without generational change, or of masses entertained with evangelical liturgies, but without making the type of disciples who fight against the kingdom of darkness and change their communities for good.

What we need to do is understand our times, sharpen our ears, and open our eyes wide. We need a humble spirit and a firm will in order to learn to expand our ministerial lungs and make the improvements that are needed.

That's what this book is about. Let us learn together!

Chapter 1

WHAT IS GENERATIONAL LEADERSHIP?

Creating a new theory is not like destroying an old barn and erecting a skyscraper in its place. It is rather like climbing a mountain, gaining new and wider views, discovering unexpected connections between our starting points and its rich environment.

Albert Einstein

For over twenty years I've been trying to learn how to influence the new generations in the name of Jesus, so it could be said that no other book I've ever had the opportunity to write has taken me as much time as this one has. Writing these pages has required me to take hundreds of trips, to study hundreds of books, and to have thousands of conversations with educators, pediatricians, hebiatric doctors, neurologists, parents, pastors, frustrated children of pastors, all types of leaders, a few crazies here and there, and many of my colleagues. But, for this book to happen, what was also needed was an interruption from God.

I like to synthesize, but I will start here because no idea manifests itself in a vacuum. There is always a story, and that story also explains a lot of the idea.

About two years before writing what you are reading, I began to feel very restless. The feeling that God wanted to tell me something began to grow in my heart, and with it a stealthy but recurring dissatisfaction in failing to discern what it was that God wanted to communicate to me.

During that time I was Zondervan´s publisher for the Spanish world, which had recently gone through a "merger" with another prestigious publisher, Thomas Nelson, and work opportunities were opening before my eyes as I had never experienced before. At the same time, our ministry continued to grow, my schedule was full, and my wife, Valeria, my children, and I were very happy. However, I could not avoid the feeling that God wanted to show me something that I still did not understand. I began to feel distracted, to lose interest in what was happening in the publishing house, and to put myself on autopilot in the ministry. I kept reading the Bible and other books, and praying normally, but I knew that something was not right. Or, perhaps, that something had to be better.

SCIENCE DOES NOT INVENT ANYTHING, BUT RATHER DISCOVERS OR MANIPULATES WHAT GOD HAS ALREADY INVENTED

As I described in detail in the book *Different*, and as my close friends know, it's been many years now that every January I practice the spiritual discipline of retreat, and I take a few days to spend in solitude and silence in order to meditate about the new year that is starting and renew my strength. As I had my retreat during this season of restlessness, and after asking the Lord many questions, I still could not discern what he wanted to tell me, but at least I understood that I had to study neuroscience again.

When I was studying for my doctorate at Fuller Theological Seminary in Pasadena, California, I took complementary courses to my doctoral dissertation at the University of California in Los Angeles (UCLA), and at Western Seminary in Holland, Michigan. My premise to do so was thinking that in order to properly serve a group of people, I should be paying attention to the details of God's design that science would have discovered about that particular group of people. My mother, who was a medical doctor, instilled in me since my childhood the idea that science does not invent anything, but rather discovers or manip- ulates what God has already invented. So I always saw science as a tool to illustrate my faith and to add effectiveness to my mission.

What I began to discover during the following months, which gave me a much broader picture of everything I had previously studied, done and learned, is what some of my colleagues and I are calling "a vision of generational leadership and discipleship."

God did not interrupt because I was doing something wrong, but because he wanted to show me something better. Do we not notice throughout the Bible that he likes to do this? God did not interrupt Mary's plans in order to get her pregnant through the Holy Spirit because she was doing something wrong. And Jesus did not interrupt Andrew and Peter by inviting them to follow him because it was wrong to fish.

THE MOST FURIOUS ENEMY OF EXCELLENCE IS BEING COMFORTABLE

God's interruptions do not necessarily come to us because we need to leave something that is wrong, but rather in order for us to embrace something better. It's not always the wrong that is the biggest threat to the best, but often the most furious enemy of excellence is being comfortable. It's doing things well.

Only well.

In recent years I realized that while knowledge is hidden in better answers, wisdom is hidden in better questions. So, for me, the vision of generational leadership began there, in that desert of new questions that leads to the promised land of new visions.

Why is it that in most of our churches, those who work with children do not have a dialogue (much less plan together) with those who work with adolescents or youth?

Why is it that in so many churches we expect the thirteen-year old to react and behave the same as the thirty-year old to the same liturgies?

Why do most pastors assume that our task is to primarily focus on the adults and that first-time leaders are the ones who need to take care of teenagers?

When does youth begin and when does it end exactly? Are we sure?

How does a preteen experience the transition from the children's ministry to that of adolescents or young people?

Why does it seem that over time it's becoming more difficult for the new generations to learn about the Bible and to embrace a faith that is not overly emotional?

Why are we unable to keep so many of the children who pass through our churches?

These are the starting questions that ignite the paradigm shift we urgently need.

A PINCH OF SCIENCE AND A SLAP TO MY MISSIOLOGY

What I rediscovered during this time of study is that, although our task is essentially spiritual, we cannot ignore the different stages of cognitive maturation, the different areas of development, and the different learning styles, because these are all variables preset by God to enable human growth. The process of maturation by which we are born as babies, become children and then move toward adulthood is not just an effect of our culture, but it is rather the art of the great artist. That is why it is so valuable to pay careful attention to these processes, if we intend to make disciples of the new generations effectively.

During those months I found an article on the subject in the *Harvard Business Review*, an article from *Time* magazine, and then some books like *The Teenage Brain* by Frances E. Jensen and "Welcome to Your Child's Brain" by Sandra Aamodt and Sam Wang and soon I was immersed in what, now I am sure, God wanted me to understand.

My neurons were stimulated by realizing that, thanks to new technology, in recent years there have been more discoveries regarding neuronal development and how the brain really works than in the previous twenty centuries. From there, God carried out his process of taking me to that desert of questions that I mentioned

OUR TASK IS ESSENTIALLY SPIRITUAL BUT WE CANNOT IGNORE THE DIFFERENT STAGES OF COGNITIVE MATURATION

earlier, and helped me to rethink my approach to working with the new generations.

These new discoveries confronted my missiology, and I became more aware than ever before of how Western our way of conceiving the church, and especially of "doing church," is.

I was able to see more clearly how the European filter, and that of modernism, colored our understanding of the mission in the Americas. I became more aware of how the flow of Christian history through Constantine and the Reformers "translated" to us a conception of ministry that is difficult to comprehend without a temple, a pulpit, and a weekly monologue about religious issues.

Complicating the picture even further, we have to add to this inheritance of ideas the fact that it's been more than half a century since these concepts were petrified, and although possibly they were relevant when they were conceived, the maelstrom of cultural and generational changes of recent years has outdated many of these premises even if they were understandable in the past.

So, *Can the ecclesiastical culture of an entire continent be changed at a specific moment in history?* It's difficult but it's not impossible. God has already made similar changes in the past, at times when some of his children stopped their ecclesiastical inertia and began asking the necessary questions.

THE FIVE STAGES AND AN INTEGRATED VISION

In the past century we learned to separate the children's ministry from the youth ministry. We learned that the youth ministry consisted of holding a meeting just like that of the adults, but on a different day and with younger participants. We finished writing in stone that the best teaching method is a monologue that should last about forty minutes on average. (I guess I was lucky with this, because in some other circles they taught that it should last at least an entire hour, in order to be biblical, or to allow the Holy Spirit the opportunity to come down, depending on whether the preacher was conservative or charismatic.) They taught us to look more at the back of people's necks than at their faces when learning from God, that the Bible is to be taught in the temple and not at home, and that questions are signs of rebellion, or can only be asked in very small groups after trust has already been established. In the English-speaking world we were taught that the goal of youth is to study at a university to make money, while in the Spanish world the goal is to get married to be happy, in both cases avoiding sin on the way to achieving these goals. And in both languages many churches taught us that the university was the enemy of our faith, or at least of the church, simply because it is usually the back door through which many children escape and stop participating.

And of course, all of this hit me hard.

After studying in one of the most popular seminars, and becoming part of the largest training organization for youth pastors in the world, I realized that I still had too many filters that wouldn't let me see the picture in all its raw beauty.

I rediscovered while seeking God by studying neuroscience and human development that there are five stages on the road to adulthood that need an intelligent pastoral and family approach from the church.

Ages 0–5, Early childhood, in which the family is the cradle of our identity and our parents are the center of our universe, or possibly the reason why we run the risk of drifting for the rest of our days. It is a stage in which the church as an institution can accompany and encourage, and yet it is very difficult for the church to compensate for what the family does or does not do.

THE CHURCH IS ALWAYS A GENERATION AWAY FROM DYING

Ages 6–9 (10), Childhood, in which our human brain is boiling with activity, and we can retain specific information as if we were investigators in a police TV series. For this reason, at this stage both the family and the church must intentionally become teachers.

Ages 11-12 (13), Preadolescence, in which abstract thinking develops while the body begins its car-racing career through a complexity of changes.

Ages 13-17 (18), Adolescence, in which our greatest vulnerabilities are expressed in order to answer the all-important question of our identity, and our friends become the mirror that defines the makeup of our values.

Ages 19–25, Youth, in which we launch ourselves toward autonomy as captains of our future.

The vision of GENERATIONAL LEADERSHIP can be summed up in developing a pertinent pastoral approach for each of these stages of development toward adulthood, with a continuous strategy instead of in isolated fragments, while planning intelligent transitions between each of these stages, and adding together the efforts of the family with those of the church.

> *I am in complete agreement with you, Lucas. Coming from a generation that precedes yours, I can say that we must honor the past and manage well the present while thinking about the future. Every leader must have a 3D vision, and this new construct that you propose hits the full target of the many different needs that up to now we have tried to address in isolation.*
>
> *- Felix*

AGING IS INEVITABLE, BUT MATURING IS OPTIONAL

The pastors of today and tomorrow need to understand very clearly that the church is always a generation away from dying. This is because God has many children, but he has never had any grandchildren. The children of Christians need to have their own personal encounter with the Lord, and, just as nonbelievers, they need to be accompanied into mature adulthood. Aging is inevitable, but maturing is optional, and we mature better when we have good role models, and when the church does its best work to teach us the values of Christ.

FOUR VISIONS OF MINISTRY TO THE FAMILY

Historically, the church of the past few centuries has approached the ministry to the family from different "macrovisions" or perspectives. These visions have functioned as frames of interpretation in defining the responsibilities of pastors, educators and leaders, and even of families, in the role of the spiritual formation of the new generations.

Obviously the variants have been many, and each denomination, congregation and family has been a microclimate, but I think that the following four descriptions help give us a complete picture.

1. THE PARALLEL PROGRAM

With the development of schooling, beginning with the influence of Switzerland's Jean-Jacques Rousseau and pushed by the French revolution, the family ceased being the primary provider of basic education. Education took place in a parallel establishment. This trend continued to increase during the industrial revolution that took place in Europe in the following years, and which also gave rise to the "Sunday school," an initiative by the Protestant churches to help those children who worked and were unable to get their basic education.

From that time on, churches in the Western world began to approach the ministry to the new generations as a parallel to secular schooling, in order to teach Bible and doctrine during the weekends. Interestingly, it was during those years that the first missionaries and the first Protestant churches began to arrive in Latin America.

Then, especially in the United States, para-ecclesiastical organizations were born that standardized the youth ministry programs, and so we arrived to the last few decades, where it is the norm that biblical education happens primarily in the temple, and that the children and youth programs in the congregation are primarily responsible for the spiritual health of the new generations, and, above all, for their biblical knowledge.

2. THE THERAPEUTIC APPROACH

The twentieth century was a time of vertiginous development that continues until today, and one of the fields of greatest progress was the study of human behaviors known as psychology. As this science gained in popularity, the importance of sharing understanding and counseling tools with families has become more noticeable, and family therapy and social psychology were born. After some years of resistance, some Christians became attracted to it, thus developing a vision that the church should offer, or at least help provide, Christian counseling to families.

Thus, in recent years it has become popular to offer conferences, congresses and symposia for the family, where those who speak are often psychologists specializing in family therapy. This has been the expertise of some parachurch organizations as well and the mindset for many churches.

From this perspective, the church cooperates by providing knowledge and counseling.

3. THE CENTRALITY OF THE NUCLEAR FAMILY

You may have heard of the "Hegelian dialectic" and I need to mention it to explain this vision. The German Gerog Hegel suggested that knowledge progresses by the proposal of a thesis that is answered by an antithesis that then creates a synthesis between both ideas, and so knowledge is built. I mention this because I believe that this perspective is an antagonistic reaction to the perspective of the parallel program.

In recent years some voices have emerged in the United States that began to speak against the separation of the different ages and the professionalization of the children and youth ministries. This perspective has not become widespread in other parts of the world yet, but it has been present on the internet in the form of sensationalist articles and videos arguing against separating children from parents for spiritual education, and stressing that discipleship is the responsibility of the family and that the Bible never mentions Sunday school, children's church or youth ministries.

The basic practical idea of this perspective is keeping together the family group for every meeting and Church activity, and there are a few denominations that do not have separate meetings based on age at all.

4. THE GENERATIONAL VISION

Thanks to new technology, today we have information that we've never had before. I'm excited when I see that the research sciences corroborate the fact that the biblical teaching models hit the mark in following God's design for the formation of new generations. Therein lies the power of this vision that combines the group and the family in the spiritual formation of the new generations.

Children, preadolescents, adolescents, and youth need strong family ties, and at the same time they also need to socialize with their peers, and to have the mentoring of close role models who will encourage them to take the next step in their maturity.

The three previous visions should not be antagonistic, but they should complement each other. It is not a choice between them, because they all have strengths, and all three are incomplete without the others.

Following is the basic diagram that illustrates the general vision of generational leadership.

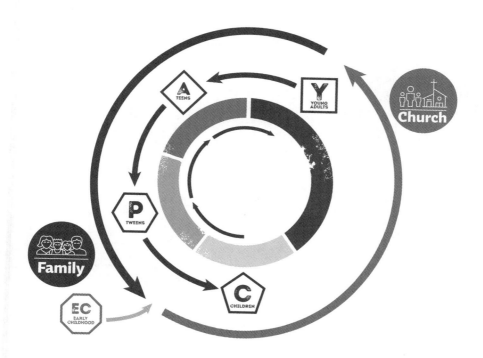

The different stages of formal education are represented in the central circle. Then there is an inner circle of arrows of influence that represents an instinctive memory installed by God, and which we will analyze in the next chapters. And in the outer circle there are the two main forces that together energize the best combination for the spiritual formation of the new generations.

Chapter 2

FOUR PARADIGMS THAT WE MUST LEAVE BEHIND

Most people catch their presuppositions from their family and
surrounding society, the way that a child catches the measles.
But people with understanding realize that their presuppositions
should be *chosen* after a careful consideration.

Francis A. Shaeffer

El Chavo del ocho used to say, "Sin querer, queriendo," which can be translated as, "Didn't mean to, but I meant to" and if you don't know the famous character from Mexican actor and producer Chespirito, then you missed out on something great in childhood.

He used that phrase when he regretted doing something that he shouldn't have done, but had wanted to do. Something like that is what happened with the European pilgrims and missionaries who expanded the evangelical faith throughout the countries in the Americas. They had the best intentions in the world, and we should be very grateful to them as heroes of the faith. But we mistakenly accepted that their ways of doing things were inseparable from our doctrine.

WE SACRALIZED THEIR FORMS

Their liturgies and their approaches to pedagogy took hold of our collective consciousness, and shaped the American and Latin American ecclesial culture. Their ways of doing things became categorical imperatives that programmed our mental structures into defining what we can and cannot do in our efforts to form disciples of Jesus.

There are many examples of this, and we could propose an academic research of each of them, but this would lead us into a different book. In this one, there are four paradigms that I want us to reconsider starting from these first pages, because I am convinced that they have been four veils that have up to now prevented us from seeing and developing an effective vision of generational leadership. These four paradigms to which I refer are the following:

- The children's ministry and the youth ministry are two completely separate ministries.

- Adults are the priority of the senior pastors.

- Ministry takes place in the church and not in the family.

- Success is measured by the number of people sitting in the Church building (temple).

These four premises have a history, and they also hide some truth, although in some circles no one is encouraged to describe them in this way or to mention them aloud. Still, they are there, in our collective awareness.

Let us then try a deeper analysis.

1. THE CHILDREN'S MINISTRY AND THE YOUTH MINISTRY ARE TWO COMPLETELY SEPARATE MINISTRIES.

I confess that for years I didn't look much at the children's ministry. My specialty and passion was always the adolescents. Even when I originally studied neuroscience, I did it to understand brain development at this stage of life, which was what interested me. Also when studying evolutionary psychology, trying to learn what this tool might suggest to me for the ministry that God had entrusted to me, I did it thinking exclusively about that transitional period that goes from childhood to adulthood, which we call adolescence.

The fact is that I was programmed to think that the ministry to adolescents should not go together with the children's ministry, because one of the basic points when working

I WAS WRONG NOT TO REALIZE SOONER THAT ADOLESCENCE STARTS IN CHILDHOOD

with adolescents was to make it clear that they were no longer children. But I was mistaken. Not because now I think that working with children is the same as working with adolescents or with young adults. It is definitely different, and in the next chapters we will address the main differences. But I was wrong to be part of creating a gap between the two stages. I was wrong not to realize sooner that adolescence starts in childhood and that childhood leads to adolescence, and that the work we do at each individual stage is incomplete if we do not coordinate it with what happens in the other.

Those who work with children and those who work with adolescents and youth can work together. Wait, let me be more specific: they must work together.

I don't mean that every week they need to meet or share activities, but they should share strategic planning, especially when it comes to the transitional periods.

This is very accurate, because changes and transitions are two different things. Scholars in the field agree that most changes fail because the transitions are not handled well. A change is an event (I turn 11 years old and I become a preteen). A transition is a process. It has to do with the loss of an identity and the birth of a new one (a change in the people with whom I study, in my activities, my interests, etc.). Something well known and loved has been lost, and what's new is yet to be configured.

> *To fail to understand this difference, and to fail to have an effect on it, is a safe bet to lose people, and even to damage them. It is during transitions that people are at their most vulnerable. In the transition to adolescence, to university, and to professional life, we lose many young people in our churches, because we do not understand and we are not paying due attention to these critical and sensitive periods of life.*
>
> **- Felix**

Have you ever asked yourself why it is that there's such a low retention rate shown by our churches, if we compare the number of children who go through our children's activities and classes with the percentage of those who remain in the church until their adolescence and youth? Clearly, one of the most notable exit doors is found precisely in the passage from childhood to preadolescence.

What happens at that moment? What happens is that they arrive at the day when they are too old to participate in the children's ministry, but at the same time the youth ministry seems to them to be an island inhabited by hairy orangutans. Naturally, they feel intimidated, and it's not surprising that they lose interest. This is especially true if we don't have a specific ministry for preadolescents, or even for adolescents and we only have a youth group without a specific age limit, which includes even those who are 30 or more as it happens in many Hispanic and African American churches!

As for pedagogy, will they now learn just as much with fewer songs? Or with more songs but in deeper voices, or with rock instruments instead of classical guitar or prerecorded music? And what exactly did they learn while they were children? During the years I worked as a youth pastor in a local church, I never took the time to find out. My thing was the weekly youth meeting and my adolescents, and I didn't realize the wasted potential of not having dialogue and strategic planning with those who worked with the children. Our efforts were disconnected. There was no correlation in learning or in experiences, and I must confess that at some point there was even competition.

(Why did the children's ministry have a budget assigned by the church, but I, as a youth pastor, had to create my own?)

Today I am a dad, and this has helped me to remember how emotional, and also how stressful, it is to pass from one stage to another. Or, to be more specific, from

TRANSITIONS ARE MOMENTS OF GREAT FRAGILITY THAT CAN OPEN OR DESTROY OPPORTUNITIES

one group to another, with different teachers, different locations and different classmates. Growing up is not easy, and transitions are moments of great fragility that can open or destroy opportunities that will change the entire course of our stories.

2. ADULTS ARE THE PRIORITY OF THE SENIOR PASTORS.

The founder of the church in which I grew up, and the one who founded the first church of your denomination, or of the denomination from which your church originated, studied at a Bible institute to teach the Bible to other adults. He simply did not have the opportunity to learn how to teach it to children or adolescents, because that was not taught in the biblical institutes at the time. The focus was adults, because that's how society was wired during the first half of the last century. This, in turn, could be said to have come from the years following the Renaissance. I mention this historical fact because it had not always been that way. If we read the Bible, we can see that during the time of Jesus, for example, the prominence of adolescents is remarkable. An obvious example is Mary who, when she was engaged to Joseph, was no more than fourteen years old, based on all the historical records of the customs of that time. Another example is Jesus' disciples. The Gospels say that Jesus was thirty years old when he began his public ministry, and according to Jewish practices about following a teacher at that time, and the descriptions of tasks and other references regarding the disciples, everything indicates that most of them were likely around or even under twenty years of age when they decided to follow the Master.

For example, in Matthew 17:24–27 Peter and Jesus discuss the temple tax that, according to Exodus 30:14, must be paid by those over twenty, and Jesus instructs Peter to "fish" for a coin and pay it. But he only mentions paying it in his own name and Peter's, although the rest of the disciples were also there. In fact, according to historians, the coin was the exact cost of the tax for two people. Why would Jesus deal only with his own tax and Peter's, but not with that of the others? The story seems to assume that others did not pay taxes, which could be a clear indicator that they were under twenty years old.

Whenever I mention this, those who listen look surprised. And I blame Leonardo da Vinci for this. The incredible Leo gave us a picture of Jesus' last supper that is full of white beards, and that has been stuck in the church's imagination for over five hundred years. Since then, we have all assumed that the disciples looked like that.

But let's return to the missionary who founded my church and yours. It was highly unusual for their wives to also study at the Bible institute. In most cases the man was the one who "had the ministry," and his wife "just came along to help him." And what could his wife do to help him? The natural thing was for her to work with the children, if they had children, and with the women, while their husbands were engaged in the ministry.

Now let's move forward one hundred years, and we can see that the profile of the vast majority of pastoral couples today remains the same. The male senior pastor teaches the Bible to adults on Sunday, and his wife works with children (if they have children or if she particularly enjoys education), or possibly she runs the women's ministry, once she has already "graduated" from the children's ministry.

This paradigm has several side effects that we will explore throughout this book, but let's start by mentioning just three.

The first effect of this model is that those who work with young people, and especially with teenagers, are new leaders, instead of being mature leaders. In the case of children, many parents naturally offer to volunteer to help in their children's meetings or in Sunday school, and we can be thankful to God that often there is also a teacher by vocation. But when it comes to working with teenagers and young people, we even experience a bit of "fear" if someone remains in the youth ministry for too long, and when they "grow up" we tell them that it is time for them to stop working with adolescents, that they'll be better off working among people their own age. Later in the book we will return to this idea.

> If you had to undergo brain surgery, what would you prefer? A young but well-intentioned surgeon or the best trained and most competent surgeon? A newly graduated doctor or someone with years of experience? Does it seem wise, then, to entrust the spiritual health of our children to people with very little experience?
>
> **- Felix**

THE VISIONARY OF THE CONGREGATION HAS AN EXAGGERATED GAP WITH THE FUTURE GENERATIOS

The second side effect of this pastoral paradigm is that the individual who drives the vision for the congregation has an exaggerated gap with the future generations that are under his or her care. They will often say, "Our young people take care of that," or "We have a couple in charge of that," but then they will complain that there seems to be a conflict of vision between the different ministries. The youth leaders have their own agenda, while the children's ministry seems to be just an afterthought, instead of being one of the main evangelistic attractions of the congregation.

The third side effect of the main pastors assuming that their ministry is only to adults, and believing that they are not primarily responsible for the ministries to new generations, is that it results in a cultural mismatch. In fact, today's average family chooses their activities based on their children, rather than basing them on their needs as parents, as was the case several decades ago. In other words, if the children are not one of the main interests of the senior pastor, this will be noticed in terms of priorities, in the budget and in the plans of the congregation, and the first ones to notice it will be children and the youth! Then, when they lose interest, sooner or later their parents will also lose interest, and that church will get old without regeneration.

TO CONSIDER THE MINISTRY OF YOUTH AND CHILDREN LESS IMPORTANT THAN THE MINISTRY WITH ADULTS IS A DEATH TRAP FOR ANY COMMUNITY

In conclusion, just for now, before my dear pastor drops this book at this very moment... am I proposing that senior pastors stop taking care of the adults? No. All age groups are vital to a healthy congregation. What I am proposing is that the main pastoral couple cannot ignore what is happening with the new generations in their congregation, and cannot consider the ministry of youth or children as being less important than working with the adults. It is true that adults tithe and adolescents and children do not, but rest assured that if those children are lost, it will become increasingly more difficult for their parents to support your vision for the church.

If Jesus chose a small group of young men and dedicated to them his three years of ministry, and worked through them to change human history, we can be sure that Jesus knew what he was doing.

3. MINISTRY TAKES PLACE IN THE CHURCH BUILDING AND NOT IN THE FAMILY.

Only a few extremely naive leaders would say this out loud, because the vast majority of us recognize that the family is the core of God's design for the healthy development of human beings. This is true even in the spiritual dimension. There can be no church without families.

However, I am not talking about what we say, but about what we do.

Although more than five hundred years have elapsed since the Protestant reform, we have not yet finished detaching ourselves from the marked "temple-ism" in our approach to spirituality. The New Testament clearly emphasizes that God does not dwell in temples made by the hands of men (Acts 17:24) and that we are the temple of the Holy Spirit (1 Corinthians 3:16), and yet we call our brick temples, made of glass and metal, "the house of God" and "the place where his presence dwells or comes." In addition, for a long time we were taught that when we go there we must dress and speak differently, because it is the one place where we must honor the Lord.

In one of the following chapters we will talk about ecclesiology, the logic of the church and what the Bible proposes as our identity and our mission as the people of God, but I didn't want to wait to mention this paradigm because it probably represents one of the areas of greatest vulnerability for the church of Christ today and this was shown in full display during the covid-19 pandemic. If our Christian families are not intentionally involved with discipleship, and if parents comfortably rest in expecting someone else at the church to teach their children to pray and read the Bible, we will unfortunately raise new generations that are weak in their faith.

> This is powerful, and it should be obvious, although it is not. We must create a strategic alliance. Parents and the church must work together in providing spiritual education to their children, clearly understanding the role that each of them must play. The responsibility of spiritual formation belongs, according to the Bible, to the parents, not to the church. The church helps with the process, but is not responsible for it. It complements, but it does not replace. Parents must not "outsource" the spiritual formation of their children to the church, and the church should not accept it when they do so.
>
> *- Felix*

Of course, all of this is understandable. One of the most notable challenges of our era is the amount of obligations that we have and the small amounts of time that we as parents dedicate to our children. Although I have always understood that it is a priority, and I can give lots of testimonies about precious conversations that I had with my children, I must also confess that I missed many opportunities due to being busy, even with church matters. And it is not because we are bad parents that we stop prioritizing the discipleship of our children. It's because we are way too busy!

The problem is that this paradigm taught us that the church is going to make things easier for us by offering programs to teach biblical principles to our children, and so we can take care of those things adults do. This idea, embedded into our awareness, comes to light when youth leaders don't pay much attention to how to involve, or how to serve, parents. We often assume that if the ministry is for teenagers, then it is just for them, and not for their parents, without realizing that the influence we can exert on our teenagers is incomplete if we do not intentionally influence the most influential people in their life as well. And, according to science, these people are none other than their parents.

> Today's parents need all the help they can get, but unfortunately, most ministerial models usually fail to offer help. At one extreme, parents are seduced to yield the spiritual development of their children to the church, and at the other extreme, less popular but also real, we shame parents by convincing them that they are solely responsible for the faith of their children. These models fail, either because we leave the parents out of their responsibility to disciple their children, or else because we simply abandon them and leave them full of guilt.
>
> - Kara

In the case of the children's ministry, the parents at least bring the children to class, and there is a little more interaction between teachers and parents. Nevertheless, the calendar of most of our children's ministries also betrays the separation between what we do at church and what happens at home. Temple discipleship

A GREAT TEAM IS REQUIRED TO ACHIEVE THE BEST RESULTS!

and family experience are two parallel and very separate realities, especially in those cases of children and adolescents with nonbelieving parents who do not even suspect that our efforts should also involve, and benefit, them as well.

I remember a pastor in Colombia who told me that his youth pastor had resigned because he no longer believed in youth ministry, since he had seen a movie that talked about how discipleship should be done by the family and not by the church. From time to time new sensationalist fashions and accusations emerge, and some sectors of the church become scandalized or fall in love with those new fashions very easily. This youth pastor had been prey to the stupor that was caused by this approach, which made him respond to this paradigm from the other end and to lose sight of the fact that, during our development, we need a specific space to share with friends and classmates. He also forgot that the church can have specialists with good resources to strengthen and enhance what is taught in a Christian home or, in some cases, to compensate or to heal what they've learned in their homes, when these children arrive in our communities hurt by their unbelieving parents. A great team is required to achieve the best results!

One of the most helpful, practical ways in which churches and families can enhance intergenerational relationships is to rethink our proportions. Traditionally, in the United States, it is thought that in the ministry we need one adult for every five children or adolescents, but what would happen if we turned the proportion around and tried to have five adults for each young person who's growing? This bold vision, initially proposed by research conducted by Chap Clark of Fuller Theological Seminary, has inspired leaders and parents to surround each student with a team of five adults who will strengthen him.

> *Who are those five? We are not suggesting that you now need to recruit five leaders of cell groups or small groups for each child or teenager. One can be the Bible school or Sunday school teacher, another can be a mentor, another one a church member who commits to pray for that child by name, another person can be an aunt who perhaps does not even attend the same congregation but decides to be one of those five people, and another may be the parents of friends of the children who decide to share in the responsibility for the spiritual health of at least one friend of their children. I have no doubt that we can help new generations reach their potential if more adults get involved in strengthening the faith of our students.*
>
> **- Kara**

In Christian families we must be very intentional in not abandoning and surrendering the discipleship of our children, just as generational ministries must be intentional in involving parents, serving and empowering them.

The church is not a fixed temple but a nomadic village. It is made up of families that help and support each other in the ways of the Lord. In some families there are doctors, in others, teachers, and in others, craftsmen. And for the village to function, everyone must be faithful in their own areas of expertise, and in turn protect those in their care. A local church is much stronger when families are healthy, and families are stronger when the rest of the members of the village complement, compensate for, and complete those families.

> *This is a key point. To try to become involved with children and adolescents in complete isolation from the systems of relationships in which they are immersed, especially without taking into account their families, is an incomplete process.*
>
> **- Kara**

We have the biblical promise: "Start children off on the way they should go, and even when they are old they will not turn from it" (Proverbs 22:6). And that instruction must be carried out in the way it was posed by the Lord in the

THE CHURCH IS NOT A FIXED TEMPLE BUT A NOMADIC VILLAGE

spectacular quote from Deuteronomy: "These commandments that I give you today are to be on your hearts. Impress them on your children. Talk about them when you sit at home and when you walk along the road, when you lie down and when you get up. Tie them as symbols on your hands and bind them on your foreheads. Write them on the doorframes of your houses and on your gates" (Deuteronomy 6:6–9).

4. SUCCESS IS MEASURED BY THE NUMBER OF PEOPLE SITTING IN THE CHURCH BUILDING.

This will be the most difficult paradigm to acknowledge. We would like to say that what we really yearn for are new converts, transformed lives, children and adolescents who will assimilate the principles of the Word of the Lord according to their ages, and university students who will decide to serve the Lord regardless of what their career is going to be and who will choose their partners well. And surely those desires exist, but I am not discussing here what we desire, but rather how we evaluate our ministerial success, both our own and that of others.

In her book *Redefining the Role of the Youth Worker*, April Diaz says: "In the context of our local church, we started to worry when we noticed how many young people were losing their commitment when they got to the university, not with our meetings, because we had already adjusted our expectations about their involvement, but rather with the decisions they were making. We concluded that we should reassess the impact of how we had discipled them in previous years, and

WHAT DOES THE SUCCESS WE ARE PURSUING ACTUALLY LOOK LIKE?

redefine what the success we were pursuing actually looked like."[1]

What does the success we are pursuing actually look like? If our mental image, when visualizing the success we are pursuing, is that of an auditorium full of people applauding how well we speak or sing, then we already know where we need to start working: we must redefine our success! That's what I did with the e625.com team. We did this exercise with the web team, with the social media team, and with our national teams that manage the training events we organize. Our first discovery was somewhat awkward. Almost all of us initially aimed for more numbers instead of for more service. Of course, the reason was not necessarily negative, and it was that an increase in the number of followers on social networks is easy to account for, but knowing who is effectively applying what we share is more complicated to measure. True, the quantitative is easier to observe and to measure than the qualitative, but we must not settle for what is easier!

We must recover, as I mentioned in my book "Every young person needs a mentor", the idea that the purpose of Jesus' coming was to make possible the new man, and the humanity that sin made unfeasible. Paul develops the concept extensively in Romans 8:28–29; Galatians 4:19; Ephesians 4:11–13; and Colossians 1:28–29, among others. The goal is to become like Jesus, Jesus shaped within us, to live and to think like the Master.

- *Felix*

We are immersed in a secular culture that is show oriented, and it has been teaching us through our senses since childhood that success is measured in popularity. And along the way, many of us swallowed that pill and became addicted to it.

---

1 April Diaz. *Redefining the Role of the Youth Worker*. The Youth Cartel, 2013.

Returning to the missionaries, I now understand the story from the other side. I know churches and associations that send missionaries to different parts of the world, and I have seen

WE MUST NOT SETTLE FOR WHAT IS EASIER

how these missionaries are expected to report the results of their work. The missionaries depend on these reports, because the church brothers and sisters who listen to them are the ones who will decide if that family of missionaries will continue to receive support for their livelihood while working in another country. In the old-school way of looking at these reports, the churches and missionary associations wanted to hear numbers, confirming the paradigm that already prevailed. How many new converts did you get in the evangelistic crusades? How many people are attending the new churches? Thank God that in recent years, missiology reconsidered the way it was evaluating the results, and today most of the churches and missionary agencies are learning to ask for fewer numbers and more stories.

Chapter 3

THE STRATEGIC VISION

*You can't depend on your eyes,
when your imagination is out of focus.*

Mark Twain

We usually use the word "administrators" to refer to those who work in finance, but the truth is that all of us are administrators.

We all manage what we have in order to produce results. And, whether we realize it or not, the results we get are the outcome of a good (or bad) administration of ideas, resources, advice and time.

The best leaders define with hawk eyes the results they are looking for, account for the available resources, and understand how these resources should interact with each other in order to produce the best results. That

> THE BEST LEADERS DEFINE
> WITH HAWK EYES THE RESULTS
> THEY ARE LOOKING FOR

is why, from this chapter on, we will work within a structure that can be easily adapted to any context, size, denomination and ministerial style, in order to enable our churches to improve their level of retention of children, impact the lives of more adolescents, and provide to our cities those disciples of Jesus who are so desperately needed.

THE GENERATIONAL VISION'S STRUCTURE

The Lord gave me the gift of allowing me to serve him in a church that had only 70 members, in another of more than 10,000 members, and of working with hundreds of congregations throughout the Americas and Europe. During all my years of experience working with local groups of different denominations and sizes, I was able to see that there are some fundamental factors in any healthy ministry, regardless of the contextual situation.

These constant factors are basic elements that are always present in our ministries. We all know that they are there, but it´s quite possible that we have not taken the time to analyze them in depth and with updated tools. Or perhaps we may have analyzed them in isolation, but without evaluating how they interact with each other in order to be able to design a structure that energizes and empowers them.

> *Over the last decade, many conferences and leadership books have highlighted time and again the importance of a clear vision. Based on the research that I have led in churches that are doing an effective job with the new generations, it was confirmed that their pastors and leaders have invested time in dreaming together and establishing a clear vision of what they are doing. When asked about the history of their churches, 31 percent of the leaders of the churches with the fastest growing new generations stated that the reason was a renewed vision of how to work with the new generations. This was the second most common response only one percent behind the assertion that a significant change in staff had been the key.*
>
> *-Kara*

In my personal history, when I got started in the ministry my focus was exclusively on what happened onstage during the meetings. Because of my own immaturity and the inconsistency of the ecclesiastical culture that I had inherited, I thought that "leadership" was to have access to the microphone and participate in decisions about who was preaching, who was leading the praise, and when and where the special activities were going to happen. Although the constant factors that we are going to analyze were present, they were in disarray. Perhaps I should even say they were abandoned, like those tools that we know we have at home but are never able to find when we need to use them.

What are the constant factors?

- Constant 1. The goal

- Constant 2. The public

- Constant 3. The leadership

- Constant 4. The relationships

- Constant 5. The programs

- Constant 6. The culture

Please note that I call them "constant" because they are always there, not because they do not change. To give two examples, the culture is always changing, and the public is always changing. What I have verified is that these elements are always present in our ministries, whether we are aware of it or not.

These six factors relate to each other in an organic and natural way, so we really don't need to do much to make them relate. But if we want them to relate in the best possible way, in order to bring our discipleship processes to the ideal level of effectiveness, then we must analyze their interaction and even foster it wisely.

The following diagram represents what we will discover together on the following pages.

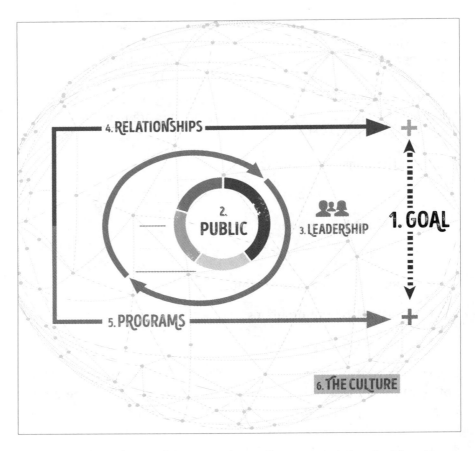

The organic dialogue between these factors reveals six keys to an extraordinary ministry to the new generations. Six devices that, when triggered correctly, will cause an expansion in our congregations.

THE 6 ACTIVE KEYS OF GENERATIONAL VISION

The constant factors are nouns, and now we are going to activate them with verbs.

KEY #1. TO FOCUS ON THE CRUCIAL GOAL OF GENERATIONAL LEADERSHIP

KEY #2. TO UNDERSTAND GOD'S DESIGN FOR HUMAN DEVELOPMENT

KEY #3. TO EXERCISE THE APPROPRIATE LEADERSHIP

KEY #4. TO DEVELOP INTENTIONAL RELATIONSHIPS

KEY #5. TO IMPLEMENT SUCCESSFUL PROGRAMS

KEY #6. TO INFLUENCE THE CULTURE

1. Effective ministries know exactly where they are going. They establish a goal, define the purpose behind each of their efforts, and set objectives for each step along the way that allows them to reach the main goal. They have evaluated and personalized what God expects from them, and they launch themselves to fulfill their role in Christ's master plan for the church, regardless of the cost.

EFFECTIVE MINISTRIES KNOW EXACTLY WHERE THEY ARE GOING

2. The new generations are the beat in generational leadership, and the central gear in the diagram. The ministry is directed toward them, with them and for them. It is done because we value them and it is not meant to meet my personal needs. It is not meant to help me

EFFECTIVE GENERATIONAL MINISTRIES ARE RELEVANT AND PROPHETIC WITHIN THEIR CULTURE

launch a career toward "the real ministry." It is not done because someone has to do it. It is not done because it's always been done, or because we need to do something with them while their parents listen to the sermons and get involved in the church.

3. Healthy ministries have healthy leaders. The best leaders are versatile enough to match their practices to each person's maturity level using different leadership styles. In healthy ministries, leadership adopts an attitude of service, develops a clear focus on the common good and facilitates a strategy that enables the desired results.

4. Effective ministries are intentional in terms of relationships. They reproduce the style of Christ, and have willing and available leaders who promote personalized contact with the children or adolescents and their families, generating an environment of acceptance and friendship in the church.

5. Excellent ministries establish the appropriate strategies to achieve the established objectives. They put aside the "it's always been done this way" mindset and replace it with methods relevant to a specific space and time. They stop the wheel of inertia and evaluate the best means to bring young people and adolescents to maturity in Christ and to achieve church growth.

6. Effective generational ministries are relevant and prophetic within their culture. They know how to differentiate between what is core and what is peripheral to the gospel, and engage in a practical dialogue with the communities they want to influence.

Mark Prensky, author of the book Teaching Digital Natives, *"indicates that for educational processes to be able to influence and have an impact on boys and girls, they must be relevant and real. "Relevant means that they are able to relate something you teach or something you say to something they know.... Real, on the other hand, means much more and goes much further. Real means that at all times (or at least as often as possible), students are able to perceive a relationship between what they are learning and their ability to make this learning useful to them in the real world."*

- Felix

Chapter 4

THE ECCLESIOLOGY OF GENERATIONAL MINISTRY

*God is not simply saving diverse individuals and preparing them
for heaven; rather he is creating a people for his name, among
whom God can dwell and who in their life together will reproduce
God's life and character.*

Gordon Fee

There is something worse than not knowing how to do things, and it is not knowing why we do them.

A few years ago I asked the following questions to a large group of youth pastors while giving a class at a respected seminar in Central America: "What would you do more often if you had all the necessary resources to do everything you dream of in your ministries?" Very quickly they raised their hands and began to share. I allowed them to take flight, and then got to the question I most wanted to ask them: "Now, honestly, why would you do that?" This time they took a few extra minutes to respond, and their faces truly reflected that they were exercising their neurons.

With this simple exercise, the fact came out that it was easy for everyone to think about innovative activities and crazy ideas, but it took a lot more work to define the why. Of course, some of them came up with Bible verses, but it became clear that each had gone in the direction that led to their own gifts and personal preferences. The evangelists cited the Great Commission, the worship leaders considered it more spiritual to spend hours in congregational singing (and of course they called it "worship"), the more intellectual ones emphasized the importance of doctrine, and those who were single thought of having more group outings.

IT IS ALMOST IMPOSSIBLE TO PUT TOGETHER A PUZZLE WITHOUT THE COMPLETE IMAGE OF WHAT MUST BE PUT TOGETHER

It is almost impossible to put together a puzzle without the complete image of what must be put together. The same thing happens in ministry. If we are not extraordinarily clear about what we must achieve, we will be entertaining ourselves by developing a program that, while possibly attractive, will not achieve lasting results in the lives of the people we wish to bless. You already know the text: "Where there is no vision, the people are unrestrained" (Proverbs 29:18).

The word "ecclesiology" may sound exuberant to some, but it simply refers to the study of the church. How is it composed? What does the Bible say about its origin, and about how it should be governed? And above all, leaving aside all religious language, for what purpose does it exist?

In practical terms, there is not a single person in the ministry who does not have at least some basic idea about ecclesiology, and it is possible that after reading the last question you may be tempted to answer it quickly. But let go of the accelerator. Give me the benefit of the doubt, and let us slowly process together what follows.

AN INTENTIONAL ECCLESIOLOGY

Each pastor and teacher has a philosophy that accompanies the ministry that he or she leads. Of course, they do not always recognize it, and the philosophy is not always organized in such a way that it can be communicated clearly.

WISDOM IS NOT OURS, BUT IS ANCHORED TO THE MESSAGE WE SHARE

Each worker is able to respond at least in an embryonic rational way to why he or she does what they do in the ministry, but it is not enough to have a vague idea. It is necessary to define where we are going in order to avoid wasting extremely valuable time with traditions, fashions or superficial expectations. And in order to accomplish this, we must go to the most reliable source of authority: the Bible.

It hit me hard when I discovered that a generational leader named Paul made a powerful statement about the goal we must pursue when working with the new generations. In his letter to the church of Colossae, he wrote: "So we tell others about Christ, warning everyone and teaching everyone with all the wisdom God has given us. We want to present them to God, perfect in their relationship to Christ" (Colossians 1:28 NLT).

It is a fabulous summary! But let's be honest. It does not seem that we always teach with all wisdom, let alone manage to make anyone perfect. So what exactly did Paul mean to say?

John Gill, who pastored the same church as Charles Spurgeon in London 100 years earlier, preached explicitly on this verse, explaining: "We teach with all wisdom when we teach the counsel of God as expressed in the gospel. When we reveal Christ for salvation, teaching them to find affirmation in His righteousness for justification, and advising them to live with sobriety and justice without respect of person, we are teaching with wisdom."[1]

---

1   John Gill. *An Exposition of the New Testament.*, 1746-48.

In other words, wisdom is not ours, but is anchored to the message we share. If what we share is based on principles of eternal revelation, it will be pure wisdom.

And perfect? The word in question in the original Greek is *teleios*, a word that can also be translated as "mature" or, as paraphrased by William Barclay, the great Scottish commentator at the University of Glasgow, "complete." The New International Reader's version translates it: to be grown up as people who belong to Christ.

THE GREAT GOAL

The summary presented by Paul shows what the great goal of the church should be when it comes to the new generations: To walk with them toward a mature adulthood. And this can only be achieved in Christ Jesus.

But what does this mean in practical terms? How do we break down that "maturity"?

Some years before writing the best-selling Christian book of the past few decades *The Purpose Driven Life*, Rick Warren and his youth pastor at the time, my friend Doug Fields, of the Saddleback Church in California, worked on the books and programs known as *The Purpose Driven Church*. With these programs and materials, Rick, Doug, and a large movement of congregations popularized the idea that the church should be focused on five purposes that emerge from the biblical texts we know as "the Great Commandment" and "the Great Commission."

In these words from Jesus we read:

"'Love the Lord your God with all your heart and with all your soul and with all your mind.' This is the first and greatest commandment. And the second is like it: 'Love your neighbor as yourself.' All the Law and the Prophets hang on these two commandments." (Matthew 22:37–40)

"Therefore go and make disciples of all nations, baptizing them in the name of the Father and of the Son and of the Holy Spirit, and teaching them to obey everything I have commanded you. And surely I am with you always, to the very end of the age." (Matthew 28:19–20)

For Rick and Doug, the principles that come to light in these verses are:

1. Worship

2. Ministry

3. Evangelism

4. Communion

5. Discipleship

As for me, and I know I am not the only one, I prefer to see communion not as an end or a purpose in itself, but as a means. Of course it is extremely important, and that is why it is one of the six main keys of this book and I will dedicate an entire chapter to it, but based on what I can observe when critically analyzing the biblical text, and from the perspective of what I have been able to notice in the ministerial execution and experience of others, I understand that communion is rather an avenue through which we reach adoration, true service, testimonial evangelism, and obedience. I have discussed this with Doug and other pastors, and that is why I break down these same texts into four sacred purposes that serve to define the goal in practical terms:

1. **Worship:** "Love the Lord your God with everything you are."

2. **Service:** "Love your neighbor as yourself."

3. **Evangelism:** "Go and make disciples."

4. **Discipleship:** "Baptizing them in the name of the Father and of the Son and of the Holy Spirit, and teaching them to obey."

SOMEONE IS SPIRITUALLY "MATURE" WHEN THEY LIVE IN AN ATTITUDE OF WORSHIP, SERVE THEIR PEERS, EVANGELIZE NATURALLY, AND CONTINUE TO GROW IN OBEDIENCE

Effective Christian leaders, whether parents, pastors, or teachers, must embrace the idea that our task is to accompany the new generations toward the maturity that expresses itself in an intimate relationship with Jesus, a genuine love for others, an enthusiasm for sharing the good news of the gospel, and a devotion for doing his will.

No one who lacks these qualities is "complete" yet, regardless of how many Christian activities they are part of, how much of the Bible they know, or how much passion they show when singing trendy Christian songs.

We could then say that someone is spiritually "mature" when they live an attitude of worship, serve their peers, evangelize naturally, and continue to grow in obedience while helping others to grow in it too, since true disciples make disciples. I am open to the idea that evangelism and discipleship can be categorized as one as they are two aspects of the same cycle.

In a later chapter we will discuss the programs, but let us stop now to consider whether our activities, liturgies, and large events achieve what we have just mentioned.

> It is important to think about this because the end never justifies the means, but always determines them! What we want to achieve will determine what means we can or cannot use to achieve it. Some means will be adequate, others neutral, and still others may be moving us away from the purpose we pursue. This is the eternal dilemma between form and function. To carry out a function (prayer) we develop a form (prayer worship service). With the passage of time, form and function get confused. And even sometimes, with the passage of time, the form ends up displacing the function.
>
> *- Felix*

Let's go a little deeper with each purpose.

PURPOSE #1. WORSHIP

All human civilizations have spoken of offering, serving and obeying their gods, but only Judeo-Christian theology insists on loving God with all that we are, because he loves humans with all that he is. In fact, separating Hebrew from Christian theology, it is notorious in Jesus' conversations and in Paul's letters that the second part of that statement only finds its full manifestation in Christ. Jesus called his heavenly Father Abba, or "daddy," and gave us the purest expression of love in his sacrifice on the cross.

Genuine worship is not about slow songs, as it is implied in so many Christian circles. It is not a musical style. It does not reduce to song, nor does it demand that we close our eyes or cry while we sing. Genuine worship is devotion of the heart that manifests itself in obedience.

> **GENUINE WORSHIP IS DEVOTION OF THE HEART, THAT MANIFESTS ITSELF IN OBEDIENCE**

It excludes fear, exacerbates trust, generates joy, and even puts us in harmony with the rest of humanity.

I truly believe it is impossible to worship without forgiving, and there are wounds that are impossible to forgive without worshiping.

When leaders tune our ministries with Christ's commandments, we work tirelessly to raise worshipers, because that is what God continues to seek. Jesus himself remembered it in John 4:23–24, when he said, "Yet a time is coming and has now come when the true worshipers will worship the Father in the Spirit and in truth, for they are the kind of worshipers the Father seeks. God is spirit, and his worshipers must worship in the Spirit and in truth."

PURPOSE #2. SERVICE

The direct consequence of loving God is to love what he loves. That is why the Great Commandment says that we must love our neighbor as ourselves. Jesus said that this would be the great sign of Christianity (John 13:35), and John exhorted us by saying that we cannot say that we love God if we do not love our brothers who are in need (1 John 4:20). Now, what does love produce in practice? Service! Of course, in saying "service" we do not mean an activity within the temple, by those who have an ecclesiastical title. Sadly, in many church circles, Christians still have a divorce—in their understanding—between service and love. For example, on the last night of many youth camps, you probably heard a call to conse-

THE DIRECT CONSEQUENCE OF LOVING GOD IS TO LOVE WHAT HE LOVES

cration. But what is communicated between the lines is that being consecrated to God must translate itself into a greater commitment to church activities, but not necessarily into a greater commitment to serve those around us or those in need. For years the church has limited "service" to what happens inside the temple. As a consequence, when children and adolescents think of "serving God," the idea many have is to handle a microphone, play a keyboard or guitar onstage, teach the Bible in Sunday school, or, at the other extreme, go to Africa as a missionary.

> *You are absolutely right, Lucas. A great follower of Jesus said that "in the needy we find Christ in disguise." My students at the university always ask me, "What will be in the exam? Under what criteria will we be evaluated?" They don't want surprises! Jesus affirmed that our final evaluation will not be about soteriology, pneumatology, ecclesiology, or the doctrine of recent times; rather, it will be about how we respond to our neighbor in need.*
>
> ***- Felix***

Effective Christian leaders understand that service is essentially love for our neighbor, and that is why they provide opportunities for the new generations to put it into practice. Service is about responding to the needs of those around us, and there are countless ways to do it. The commander in chief entrusted us to raise a generation of servers, and we must use our best strategies to achieve it!

Many young people in our churches want to make a difference, and all our congregations have the power to facilitate it, especially helping them to understand the reason for their passion by connecting their yearning with the gospel's redemption narrative. For upcoming sermons, series or classes, let's think actively about how we can inspire teenagers and emerging adults to be the best neighbors in their communities and to see that desire in connection with God's original plan.

- Kara

PURPOSE #3. EVANGELISM

I am not talking specifically about your congregation, but if you travel like me, you will realize that if there is something we talk about a lot and practice very little, it is evangelism.

I can think of three reasons for this.

The first one is that we see evangelism as an activity we do at a specific point in time, rather than as a purpose in which we should focus all our efforts.

The second is that we have a very "formulaic" idea of how to do evangelism, and we have turned it into something that "evangelists" do instead of considering it a natural testimony that all of us can give.

The third is that perhaps we need more compassion for those who are losing both a heaven on earth and an eternal heaven in glory with Jesus.

HEALTHY MINISTRIES DO NOT OFFER EXCUSES FOR THE STAGNATION OF A CONGREGATION

Healthy ministries do not offer excuses for the stagnation of a congregation. We must raise new generations who are enthusiastic about evangelism and who understand that it is not a negotiable variable in the Christian experience. Not for the lost, and not even for themselves.

The purpose of evangelizing should permeate every activity in our ministries to the new generations. If we want joyful and contagious children, preteen, adolescent and college ministries, then we must point all components toward an outgoing ministry continually focused on sharing the good news of Jesus.

PURPOSE #4. DISCIPLESHIP

DISCIPLESHIP IS A PROCESS OF LOVE

Discipleship is a process of love. It can start very early in life, and it will end in heaven. You are reading this book because you have a special interest in having children, adolescents or young people learn to obey Jesus and always keep growing in their faith. What is the use of having a "successful" ministry of children or preteens if in a few years those young people are not going to be obeying Christ? The goal is not to have a church full of children who know how to speak the "evangelical" dialect.

The well-known thinker Henri Nouwen used to emphasize that "disciple" and "discipline" are the same word. Being disciples and friends of Christ means that we want to live as he taught us. Discipleship is not a program or a method. Discipleship means practicing the disciplines of Christ to the point that our life infects others with the obedience they can see in us. That is why in a few pages we will analyze specifically the type of leadership we need to develop. We must live the teachings of Christ to be able to model them to those we lead. Some of these teachings are to love without conditions or preferences, resist temptation, help the needy, and always keep in mind our values. This is an incredible responsibility when working with new generations, especially considering the ecosystem in which we are entering.

Christ practiced retreat, prayer, mercy, forgiveness, simplicity, compassion, and sacrifice and we must teach all this by being involved in the same disciplines in which Jesus was involved.

THERE IS NEVER A TIME WHEN IT IS NOT IMPORTANT FOR ALL INVOLVED TO UNDERSTAND THE GREAT REASON FOR WHAT WE DO

In other words, attaining to the whole measure of the fullness of Christ (Ephesians 4:13), not being like children in understanding (1 Corinthians 14:20), taking hold of that for which Christ Jesus took hold of us (Philippians 3:10), wanting to know Christ (Philippians 3:10) and grasping together with all the Lord's holy people how wide and long and high and deep is the love of Christ (Ephesians 3:18), must constantly be targeted by our ministries.

CONTINUOUS COMMUNICATION

The next step, after clearly establishing the goal, and the purposes that explain it, is to communicate them intelligently. Those who do a better job know that people understand the mission of a team in many different ways, so they make sure, in different ways, that as many people as possible of those involved are clear about where they are going.

For example, it is a fact that some of us are more visual, while others are more conceptual, and there are even those who are only mobilized by emotional ties. That is why it is necessary to use various methods to strengthen the direction of our ministries.

The careful use of words, images, and symbols is an art known as "semiotics" and, although we may not use that word, it is a vital component in any healthy social group.

There is never a time when it is not important for all involved to understand the great reason for what we do, whom we work for, and what promises are at stake. Three secrets that I have seen work over the years for effective communication are:

- ✓ Personalize
- ✓ Repeat
- ✓ Evaluate

PERSONALIZE

We all, even children, need to know why we are in a certain place and why we are doing a certain activity. Children despair when they don't know the purpose of something; adults do too, but we've learned to camouflage despair at Church. Or perhaps we got used to it.

Nowadays it is very rare to walk into an important corporation and not find in the reception area a large picture that highlights the mission statement of that company. The most prominent multinationals on the planet have learned the importance of having not only their CEOs and vice presidents know their mission, but also each of their employees should know what the end result of their efforts is.

Why? Because the better we understand the reason for an activity, or even for a rule, and the clearer we can see the results of fulfilling it or not, the easier it becomes to carry out the activity or comply with the rule with enthusiasm. This truth applies to children, adolescents, and university students, to parents, and also to the team of leaders. That is why it is important to ask yourself in relation to your church: *Do we have a mission statement in our ministries to the new generations?* How about writing one soon, or reviewing what you already have, after reading the next chapters? (The next chapter will bring you plenty of light in terms of the integrated vision mentioned at the beginning of the book.)

A mission statement does not have to include elaborate words or explicit Bible verses. The statement should simply summarize what is understood to be God's purposes for that particular church or organization.

> My personal mission statement is: "Help leaders and organizations realize their full potential." The mission statement of the church that I pastor is: "Be agents of restoration and reconciliation on behalf of God in the city of Barcelona." Our mission is important because it is our perennial reason for being, our unique and extraordinary contribution to the kingdom of God.
>
> **- Felix**

Worship, service, evangelism and discipleship, and even the great commandment and the great commission, must be present, but it should not be literally every word. Why? Because it should feel personal; something that's our own, not something universal. In fact, using these specific words creates an extra challenge, since the ideas people have of them don't always match exactly what the Bible says and what we understand when using them.

Customizing has the great benefit of allowing identification. The mission statement must have a personal and a joint meaning in the life of the members of the group that launches the mission. That is why it is better to write it

CUSTOMIZING HAS THE GREAT BENEFIT OF ALLOWING IDENTIFICATION

in our own words although this is not just about wording because you can include design, color and even textures in this exercise.

In doing so we should avoid using exaggerated phrases, which eventually become unrealistic and end up causing frustration; it becomes something so huge that it is not even worth trying. I mean phrases of the type: "Our purpose is to impact the world!" I mean, does a local church intend to impact the entire planet Earth? What exactly does it mean? The people who don't know God? And how are we going to do that? If we want to include geography, then it is better to start with our town or our city or, being very ambitious, our country or continent, but in that case we better be sure that this is what God intends for us to do.

Recently I received a press release from a young pastor from a Latin American country who said in his biography that he was someone who "was impacting his country." I was interested to know more about him, but I discovered that not even the pastors in his city knew him, that his ministry was just beginning, and that his newsletter (which was the basis on which his ministry was being built) had an output of 2,000 copies, in a country of several million. It is always a good idea to be humble and focus on the place where God has put us.

One last piece of advice, but a very important one: Let's not make the mission statement alone. We have to involve as many people as possible in the process, even if it becomes slower and more tedious than deciding on our own. Discussing the mission statement is developing the core of your brand and is a precious opportunity to get everyone to focus on the great goal and its purposes.

REPEAT

Almost every time I start a meeting with one of our teams, I begin by verbalizing the goal we pursue, even if it is a team I work with continuously. What I have learned is that this habit synchronizes the attention of individuals. Hearing the reason we are gathered, the distractions are minimized. Doing this, I manage to capture the attention of the group, because it's one thing for them to have to listen to me, and another to want to do it. We must remember that forgetting the reason behind each one of our efforts is much more common than we usually assume.

> *On my bad days I go to meetings with a mental score card. How many good ideas do I have today? Am I among the 50 percent of people who contribute to the meeting, or the 50 percent who have nothing to contribute? On my good days, on the other hand, I go to meetings with a disposition to help the community. I have noticed that this happens much more often when the purpose of that meeting is fresh in my mind.*
>
> *Every person and every idea is valuable because everyone contributes to the community when there is a precise mission. An idea that at first glance does not sound so good can create an amazing brainstorm in another person. A small idea, even if it does not appear to be any good, can be the spark that ignites a fire of brilliance in others, and from that perspective all contributions are equally important, because we are not at the meeting to fulfill out individualistic purposes, but to develop a shared conscience.*
>
> *—Kara*

We all know churches and institutions that started with a purpose in mind and then, as the years went by, forgot what they existed for. Surely you know denominations that began in order to wake up the rest of the church, and now are among those that are most asleep. What happened? They forgot why they existed, or perhaps they existed for temporary rather than eternal purposes, like the great commandment and the great commission.

I know many ministries that at the beginning of the year set annual goals with a prophetic word or rhema, depending on the context, and remind everyone of their purposes, but then after a few months they forget what they expected to achieve. Then what happens the rest of the year loses connection with what they had proposed at the beginning. Why does this happen so often? In many cases it is a lack of clarity but quite often it is just the lack of repetition. It is necessary to keep repeating the mission statement and core beliefs in different ways throughout the year.

It's been proven that human beings have different ways of learning, but nevertheless I still get surprised at how people much smarter than I am, with whom I work continuously, need to be reminded of why we do what we do, or why we do it in a certain way, and not as other ministries do it.

In addition, the different personality types usually connect to the mission statement in different ways. That is why it is important to repeat the personalized mission statement in various ways, taking this fact into account. The images are going to help those who are visual, the preaching and songs are going to help those who are auditory, and the personal conversations are going to help those who are affective. There are many people who, unless told by someone they trust in an intimate way, will never really commit themselves to the mission. This is especially true in the case of children and adolescents, due to the stage of cognitive maturation in which they are.

What can we do to repeat the goal, its purposes and our mission continuously?

- Videos to spread virally

- Posters

- Theme songs

- Put the statement on paper and letterhead

- Dedicate one month of the year to remembering it

- Read it before leaders' meetings

- Repeat the mission statement when starting the service

- Use live dramas or do a short film

- Post it in church bulletins

- Periodically interview someone who has done something meaningful that illustrates a purpose accomplished and its benefits

- Paint it on a wall

- Banners

- Email signature

- Bookmarks

- Have children make posters completing the mission statement

- Have young people give testimonies about the results

- Voiceover to proclaim it

- Debates

- T-shirts

- Bracelets

And surely you know other ideas about how to do it.

EVALUATE

When I finished high school I was terrified of going to the dentist. My mother insisted that I go, but I always figured out a way to avoid it. My best excuse was that the last time I had gone, my dentist had not found anything wrong and had told me that my mouth was perfectly healthy. The logical rules of prevention say that you have to go to the dentist at least once a year for an evaluation to keep cavities under control, but I stopped going for almost three years... until I felt some pain. When my dentist checked me after such a long time, he found a tooth decay zoo. My teeth, which until the previous evaluation had been in perfect condition, were never the same again, and to this day I am paying the consequences for those three years during which I neglected my dental evaluation.

Evaluating yourself can be uncomfortable, but it is crucial.

> *Albert Einstein said, "Insanity is doing the same thing over and over again and expecting different results." Greek philosophers claimed that a life not examined was not worth living. And Psalm 139 invites us, in its final verses, to incorporate into our lives the habit of being evaluated by God. We always start our team meetings with three evaluation questions: 1. What have we done well since we last saw each other? 2. What should we improve? 3. What should we do differently?*
>
> **- Felix**

I do not like generalizations, but let me speak of my culture. One observation with which many cultural observers agree is that Spanish speakers do not find self-criticism easy. All Spanish-speaking societies have experienced times of autocratic national leadership during which we were unable to object to anything, and we lived in environments where disagreeing with an idea was seen as a threat to the system or as a sign of rebellion.

We must correct that, regardless of culture.

And I don't want you to think that this isn't difficult for me. *Why do I insist that it is important?* Because having our goal and its purposes very clear, and personalizing this vision in our own individual mission statement, not only leads our efforts in the right direction, but also facilitates the possibility of measuring the results. And as we evaluate, we also refine the vision and the effectiveness of our initiatives.

Some important questions to ask ourselves periodically are:

What purpose are we going to be achieving with this program?

Is there any purpose that is being neglected in our programming?

Which individuals are best at covering each of our purposes?

Is there a better way to optimize the results by doing something we haven't tried yet?

Is there evidence that we are helping new generations to mature?

Measurement has been a troublesome thing for the church for two thousand years but, again, effective ministry is not about doing what is easy. Many Christian organizations are unclear about what data is meaningful to their ministry and that again highlights the vitality of knowing your goal and breaking it down in atemporal purposes. The next step is being honest about whether we find stories that corroborate what is really happening in the lives we are affecting. Again, numbers are a factor but they do not tell the whole story, so let's ask God for spiritual discernment and let's rest sure that evaluating is a crucial practice of healthy ministries.

Chapter 5

THE FIVE STAGES ON THE ROAD TO ADULTHOOD

The first demand any work of art makes upon us is surrender.
Look. Listen. Receive.

C. S. Lewis

To share a class with eight-year-old boys is a challenge. They interrupt. They make comments about the lesson without any editing. They release "scientific" details that have no apparent connection. They collect things while they listen. They show them to the person next to them. They ask for water. They remember some superhero. They ask to go to the bathroom because they drank water. They look out the window, and if there is no window, they look at that strange illustration on the wall. Is it a giraffe, or an unknown dinosaur? They answer a question, but that was not the answer to that question but something else that came to their mind and had nothing to do with the lesson. And... did I say that they interrupt?

Eight-year-old children are a work of art. I know it because at some point I was eight myself, because not long ago my son was eight, and because I also taught classes to children who were eight. And just as there are people who run a cold sweat if they have to speak in public before a large group of people, that same cold sweat runs through me if I have to teach a class to eight-year-old children.

JUST AS HE PAINTS COLORS IN THE SKY IN THE EVENING, THE CREATOR OF THE WORLD DESIGNED A PATH OF GRADUAL MATURATION

Each stage of life is crucial, and generational leadership is precisely about respecting each individual stage and understanding every single one in connection to the others.

The very fact that there are stages is part of the design of the great celestial artist. Just as he paints colors in the sky in the evening, the creator of the world designed a path of gradual maturation, a cycle for life. And the better we understand this cycle, the more effective we will be at getting the most out of it.

THE DIFFERENT STAGES FROM THE CHURCH'S PERSPECTIVE

Too many children and young people lose their opportunity to enjoy the unconditional love of God, a dynamic relationship with Jesus, and the vitality of a healthy Christian community. That is why the second key of generational leadership is to understand God's design for human development. We must understand this audience if we want to serve them in the best possible way and accompany them toward the great goal and their purposes.

Let's look at the 5 critical stages of development in greater depth:

- Early childhood
  - Childhood
    - Preadolescence
      - Adolescence
        - Youth

AGES 0–5: EARLY CHILDHOOD

Children under five need their parents. They need them, without question.

Pastors and church leaders must understand that during this stage these parents cannot have another priority ahead of spending time with their small children.

These parents are going to be late for meetings.

These children are going to make annoying noises and offer us strange smells when we are with their parents.

These families are going to have to make a great effort to ensure that the story of that child begins with a great start.

The human brain is a mysterious universe and, to the surprise of science, the possibility of "seeing" and "reading" the movement of neurons has advanced faster than even the most prominent scientists could have anticipated only a few years ago.

Today we have electroencephalo-grams, magnetoencephalography, positron emission tomography, functional magnetic resonance imaging, and nuclear magnetic spectroscopy, all of which allow us to verify that the brain is continually reorganizing itself. This is called "neuroplasticity."

EVERYTHING THAT HAPPENS BEFORE THE AGE OF FIVE ACCELERATES OR SLOWS NEUROPLASTICITY FOR THE REST OF LIFE

Everything that happens before the age of five accelerates or slows neuroplasticity for the rest of life. In simpler words, the first five years of life have much more to do with our intelligence than we ever knew, and they also have a lot to do with the healthy regulation of our emotions.

THE LOCAL CHURCH HAS TO BE VERY ATTENTIVE TO SINGLE PARENTS, INCLUDING THOSE WHO ARE WIDOWED OR DIVORCED

Dr. David A. Souza, author of the influential book *How the Brain Learns*, states, "The window to develop emotional control opens between two and thirty months. During this period, the limbic (emotional) system and the frontal lobe where reasoning works are each evaluating each other's ability to allow their owner to get what they want. It is an unfair competition, since today we know that biological growth occurs faster on the sides than on the front. Consequently, the emotional is more likely to impose itself on the rational in the war for control, and this is where, if the unsuspecting parents allow the child to always get what he wants by manifesting an emotional outbreak or a 'tantrum,' they are confirming that system, and that will be the system that the child will most frequently use after the window closes."

This is an amazing example of how the education provided by our family can influence our nature for life, and why it is so vital that parents focus on their parenting task.

Another incredible aspect at this stage is the acquisition of language and vocabulary. Several studies confirm that children whose fathers speak to them more often have more complete vocabularies. The linguistic areas of the brain are activated between 18 and 20 months. At age three we can learn ten new words per day, and by age five we have a vocabulary of close to 3,000 words. Then the neuronal slow-down of language gradually begins.

By the end of this stage, children are able to put together complex phrases, and mix fantasy and reality in very funny ways. Some even speak for a long time, just because of their need to communicate.

At this stage, each family needs the understanding of their Christian community. They need pastors, leaders and friends who continually validate them as parents, and who do not add additional reasons to distract them as parents. This will help them avoid becoming those who, due to other "good" activities, miss out on their opportunity to fully exercise their fundamental role of intentionally shaping the nature of their children.

The local church has to be very attentive to single parents, including those who are widowed or divorced. It is not enough to be attentive in the church. The direct influence we can have on children at this stage is limited, but the influence we can have on them through their parents or their intimate family circle is extremely powerful.

AGES 6–10: CHILDHOOD

Statistics highlight the fact that those children who have a greater number of adults positively involved in their lives are more likely to succeed in adulthood. During this phase, parents remain the children's main influence, but the other relationships in their lives begin to have a growing impact.

Children need stable relationships to be able to learn to not discard relationships based on circumstances. One example of this is the **CHILDREN WHO HAVE A GREATER NUMBER OF ADULTS POSITIVELY INVOLVED IN THEIR LIVES ARE MORE LIKELY TO SUCCEED IN ADULTHOOD** figures from various studies that confirm that children who experience the divorce of their parents during this phase greatly increase their own chances of also getting divorced as adults.

During this stage children begin to investigate the rules, and a sense of justice begins to stand out in their reasoning. Gifts must be distributed equally. The rules should apply in the same way to everyone. If it does not work that way in school or at church, they will lose confidence that the church and the school are safe places where they will want to spend their time.

The differences between people begin to be more than mere details. After age seven, the world stops being only about nouns, and now begins to have many adjectives. Poor, rich, cute, ugly, intelligent, dumb, tall, short, athletic, slow... begin to be labels. There is still not much room to investigate what is behind them, but these differences begin to create perceptions about how we are to treat each other.

A very common mistake in many congregations is to pretend that the same teaching or pedagogical methodology that we use with adults can also work well with children, if only we change the songs, decorate the classrooms with bright colors, and modify the "tone" that we use when teaching. Frankly, I am surprised when visiting some megachurches in the United States, and I notice that the children's classes were the same as the adult meetings, except for those "special effects."

Children are not "mini adults" and having a roller coaster decoration on the ceiling and a lot of children because there are a lot of adults in the main auditorium do not equate to having an effective kids' ministry.

During this stage, children have the ability to retain concrete information in a way that we will never have again, and that is why childhood presents a colossal opportunity to teach the Bible and some of the fundamental doctrines of the faith. The children's ministry should not be only a time for us to take care of them while their parents attend the "real" meetings. As in their secular education, in their spiritual formation there must also be a teaching program with clear learning objectives, and a panoramic vision of what we are teaching.

In addition, between ages 6 and 9 we all are a bit like scientists. We look forward to discovering how things work. We have a desire to learn, but we need repetition. And we need to have a clear application of what we learn in order to connect it effectively to our behavior.

David Kolb, an educational researcher who has greatly influenced the educational theories that shape elementary school teachers in the United States, proposes a four-instances learning cycle to teach children effectively.[1]

---

1   David Kolb. *Experiential Learning: Experience as the Source of Learning and Development.* Englewood Cliffs. NJ: Prentice Hall, 1984.

The four items below must show a circular motion.

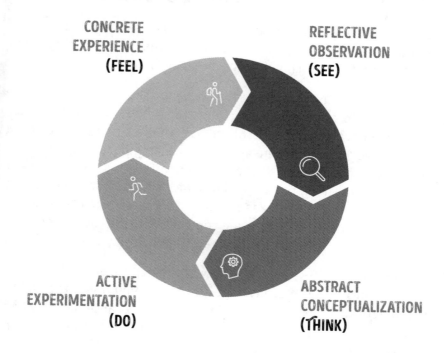

For children to learn, it is not enough that they hear the right information. They need to touch, see, question and think about what we are telling them. Later we will expand this proposal by talking about programs and relationships.

Every parent in the world is interested in having their children at this age learn the right information when it comes to math, language, history, geography and science. As Christian parents we also want them to learn about the Bible. But what all parents truly want, Christian or not, is for our children to learn to be responsible, hardworking, sensitive, compassionate and disciplined.

The church, then, at this stage must connect the biblical stories with God's principles for life, precisely because they have the power to unleash the best capabilities in human behavior.

AGES (10) 11–12 (13): PREADOLESCENCE

The main corporations behind fashion, electronics and audiovisual media are very interested in this stage of life. It's as if they know something that in our churches we are unaware of.

In the field of philosophy and in the academic sector, where they like to put labels to generations, it is debated whether preadolescence is a consequence of postmodernism. But whether there is a cultural effect involved or not, there is truly an emerging stage, different from adolescence—since it precedes puberty—and also different from childhood. In English the boys at this stage are known as "tweens," making a pun between "teens" (teenagers) and "between." This refers to the fact that they are too mature to be considered children, but they are still too young to be called teenagers.

Today, thanks to CT scans, we know that just before puberty the brain goes into a frenzy of massive growth, adding millions of additional neurons. The emphasis is on adding, because later, when puberty arrives, the process is reversed, and during the next two to four years, during adolescence, the brain is reduced by millions of neurons. Amazing, right?

Obviously, this detail is not an effect of postmodernity. Rather, it is evidence that God has a special plan for this phase of life. When neurons are grouped together, they are called "neural pathways," and they become the superhighways of information that the brain manages. As we have already pointed out, the acceleration they manifest during this phase is remarkable.

In a few pages we will expand on the fact that preadolescence is when abstract thinking begins. Preadolescents begin to think in critical terms about themselves. When they were entering childhood, they believed that they were great at whatever they wanted to be. They could draw like Picasso and run like Usain Bolt. But now they begin to have the opposite feeling. There are very few preadolescents who do not doubt themselves. They begin to realize that there are different perspectives of reality, and in doing so they may become disillusioned and feel confused. They discover that there are different worldviews from that of their family, and that the values of their group are not the same as everyone's, including those of good people whom they respect. (They ask themselves, "How can it be that good people think like that?")

From the perspective of the parents and the church, it is very important to know the two questions that head the entire list of questions that preadolescents ask themselves during this stage: "Who likes me?" and "Who do I like?".

But a word of warning: These two questions are not synonymous with "Who loves me?" And "Who do I love?" It would be great if by this time they already knew that they are loved by God, by their parents and by the church. But at this point they are searching for something else. They want "reasons" that go beyond, for example, "My parents love me because I am their daughter"

At this stage we need to give our preadolescents pure, direct and continuous affirmation. Unapologetically.

AGES 13–17 (18): ADOLESCENCE

Puberty marks the entry into adolescence. From the Latin "pubescere," the word indicates the appearance of pubic hair. The biological alarm sounds, and the genital organs wake up. Guys and girls, surprised, are filled with curiosity and want to know what is happening to them.

It is a biological fact that puberty is now coming at younger ages. Historical documents indicate that centuries ago it occurred at fourteen or even sixteen years of age, and today it happens around twelve years of age and is already established at thirteen. Of course this can vary from person to person, and there are differences between girls and boys. But in both, the body begins to take its adult form. Girls see their hips widen and boys their shoulders. Although the apex of adolescence is about sexual development, the voice also changes and, above all, we grow in stature due to elongations in the skeleton (something that in my case didn't happen enough).

But the external changes that occur in adolescence are initiated on the inside, in the endocrine system. The process begins when the hypothalamus, part of the brain, instructs the pituitary gland to activate the adrenal glands and gonads (ovaries or testicles).

The gonads produce testosterone in men, and estrogen and progesterone in women. These are responsible for the differentiation of the reproductive system and, in the case of estrogen and progesterone, they are responsible for regulating the menstrual cycle.

From the perspective of the family and the church, this is the stage in which we should channel that desire to differentiate ourselves while feeling the pressure not to be excluded. The best leaders of adolescents repeat the word "potential" over and over, because this is the great practical key to working with teenagers. This is the phase in which we unwrap the gift, uncover the bottle, and start offering the world that perfume that only an individual can offer.

The big question during adolescence is, "Who am I?" We will later analyze it in more detail, and there are other questions that are also important, such as: "Where do I belong?" "What should I believe, and why is it so difficult for me?" "Why do I matter?"

> This is an excellent list of concepts and questions, and I want to highlight one aspect. Different statistics show that only one of seven students finishing high school feel prepared for college.
>
> According to what adolescents say, most feel that their preparation to be successful in college and in life is poor. This is a detail that we should keep in mind, because studies confirm that this feeling is a factor in their performance in college and even in life. When considering the transitions as this book is proposing, this is not a minor detail as we accompany them correctly to the next stage.
>
> -Kara

AGES 19-25: YOUTH

This is the stage they all looked forward to and dreamed about since preadolescence, but now it is no longer about dreaming it but living it. And, above all, it's about decisions. Everything now goes through personal decisions. Vocation, sexuality, partner, economics, and faith suddenly become competing forces.

With age eighteen comes a new practical independence and also adult obligations, and even if they still want to be teenagers, at church we must learn to accompany them wisely. The church cannot treat them as teenagers, nor expect them to commit themselves as they did when they went to high school and were protected by law as minors. Yet we cannot think of them as fully adults yet.

For hundreds of years it was thought that brains were fully formed since childhood (from around age six, to be exact, according to many scientists of yesteryear). After that, all that was left was to learn content, grow a little in size, and certainly also in speed, functionality and emotional intelligence. But basically we were convinced that everything was already there, and it just had to grow. We did not suspect that we were wrong.

BRAINS ARE NOT FULLY FORMED UNTIL AROUND TWENTY-FIVE YEARS OF AGE

When MRIs and diagnostic imaging allowed medicine to see brain activity in real time, it was a great shock to discover that brains are not fully formed until around twenty-five years of age! Before that age, there are vital parts of the brain that are literally absent, and there are others that are still developing.

When our ministry team began to talk about these findings and then about generational leadership, and to share that we should "graduate" the young people toward adulthood, and we decided strategically to work with children from age six to young people of age twenty-five, excluding those who are past that age, a strong point of discussion was generated within my team. The usual view of youth ministry in most Hispanic churches is to include all singles no matter what age they are, and I found an echo of that in many African American churches as well. In most churches of the United States, by contrast, the tendency is to be unconcerned with those over 18, assuming that they now belong to the adult world or at least to the university world and that they return to their congregations as adults when they return from college.

WE CANNOT BE COMPLICIT IN THE ADOLESCENTIZATION OF CULTURE, AND THE IMMATURITY OF MANY

If, according to our brains and even our endocrine system, we reach adulthood at twenty-five years of age, this is by God's design. If the fabulous biology designed by God indicates that at age twenty-five there are hormonal and cellular changes, and even our brains reach their peak of formation and a deceleration in learning begins, even though the brain has reached its biological maturity, why then be complicit in the adolescentization of culture, and the immaturity of many who prefer to live until way past their thirties with Peter Pan syndrome?

Also, think about this carefully. Why does saying that youth ends at age twenty-five sound like bad news in some circles?

Where do we get that idea?

It was the consumer society that in recent decades became infatuated with implying that we should look like adolescents, although it demands an increasing number of surgeries.

Young people are gregarious, prefer intimacy and conversations, and need more space. Reaching that stage should not be seen as bad news and leaving it much less. Our churches must be a springboard that propels new generations into mature adulthood. I insist. Why should it be considered bad news to reach another stage designed by God, and especially that particular stage in which maturity is established and we can leave a legacy?

What happened is that we unconsciously accepted the lie from the consumer society. The ideal is not to always have an adolescent body, use their fashions, and live eternally in a rock star's style. If God's plan is for us to become adults, then becoming adults is wonderful!

Young people from age 19 to 25 are making the decisions that will condition the rest of their lives. They need to leave adolescence and move toward full adulthood but they shouldn't do this alone and unguarded by their faith communities.

OUR CHURCHES MUST BE A SPRINGBOARD THAT PROPELS NEW GENERATIONS INTO MATURE ADULTHOOD

An alarming statistic indicates that only 20 percent of college students who abandon the faith claim that they suspected during high school that they would do so. The other 80 percent confess that during high school they were sure that they would keep their faith forever, but they lost it at the university because at this stage they felt abandoned by their churches.

-Kara

THE FIVE TRACKS OF DEVELOPMENT

Throughout this path to adulthood, human beings begin to develop our unique and independent identity different from that of our parents. Identity becomes the great objective of our development, and it manifests itself visibly in the body and also in our emotions, in our social sphere, in our intellect and in the spiritual realm.

Properly interpreting what happens to new generations in their inner self is essential to be able to practice intelligent discipleship. That is why we insist on asking:

What is happening in their brains as they develop?

Why do they express their emotions in that way?

How can they really experience God at the stage they are in? And what is the best way to help them do it?

We usually catalog each other based on what happens in everyone's sight, but understanding people's inner self is the secret of the wise.

PROPERLY INTERPRETING WHAT HAPPENS TO NEW GENERATIONS IN THEIR INNER SELF IS ESSENTIAL TO BE ABLE TO PRACTICE INTELLIGENT DISCIPLESHIP

Adults usually spend hours in phone calls and conversations discussing whether or not the younger people behave well at the meetings, how they dress, the words they use, and where they like to go out at night, in the case of the older ones, instead of discussing the inner issues that are the most important, and which result in them doing what they do.

The best leaders understand that the maturation process is integral. And the race toward adulthood runs through the 5 tracks of development:

- Physical
- Intellectual
- Emotional
- Social
- Spiritual

In each of these tracks there are factors unique to each stage that are very valuable secrets for our work.

PHYSICAL

The old Greek ascetics were wrong. God created the human body. And if God created it, then the human body is not essentially evil or opposed to spirituality.

> *That's right, Lucas. And let us not forget the incarnation of Jesus. God, taking human form and becoming as one of us, honored our body and showed us that there is nothing wrong with it. The incarnation of Jesus has always been scandalous, even for some of the early Christians. Docetists, as early as the end of the first century, denied that Jesus' body was real, because they could not accept the idea that God would take a human body, since they considered the body evil.*
>
> **- Felix**

Just because the aim of this book is the spiritual formation of the new generations does not mean that understanding the changes that take place in our body is not important. The body is always the most visible part of who we are, and the changes that we go through during each stage are part of a battle with extraordinary consequences. In addition to bodily health, we must add aesthetic acceptance, and in a culture as demanding toward our body as today's Western society is, everything that happens to the body affects our moods, our assessment of our identity, and our self-confidence.

In his book *Developmental Psychology*, the distinguished professor of psychology David R. Shaffer states: "Many factors affect growth and physical development. Among the biological contributors are genotype, maturation, and hormones. But in addition, proper nutrition, good health, and the absence of prolonged emotional trauma are necessary to ensure normal growth and development."

Our environment and circumstances also affect physical development. Healthy nutrition is not a minor detail. The Christian family and the church must be attentive to this factor in order to ensure integral health and maturation.

INTELLECTUAL

Some call this track "the cognitive area," and throughout this book you will see that I refer to the importance of understanding the maturation processes the brain experiences, because this is where we make the decisions about what we believe and what we do.

The brain is the most powerful muscle a person has. It is our most sensitive sexual organ, our true source of creativity, and even our true "heart," because when we talk about our emotions we are not talking about the device that pumps blood through our veins.

Intellectually healthy children will ask many questions.

Intellectually healthy preadolescents will insist on knowing what their relationship is with things.

THE BRAIN IS THE MOST POWERFUL MUSCLE A PERSON HAS

Intellectually healthy adolescents will be open to new ideas. Their ability to reflect in the abstract, combined with the fact that they still don't have strong opinions based on experience, results in exactly the right formula for an age of intellectual adventure. That's why teenagers love to dream, and at the same time criticize so much.

Intellectually healthy youth will want to act out of personal convictions. Autonomy of opinions is at this stage more urgent than ever in order to reach mature adulthood.

And all the new generations have a great deal of respect for the truth. When we know how to motivate them, their search for truth can be fascinating. Acquiring knowledge, developing value judgments, forming moral behaviors, and evaluating ethics are all fundamental aspects of their intellectual development.

Interestingly, many experts in the subject of education of the new generations affirm that we should ask children and young people more questions, and give them less answers to questions that they do not ask themselves. It is worth reading what Prensky and Vella wrote about this topic.

- Felix

EMOTIONAL

Immature people live constantly trying to prove that they have value, and often suffer extreme changes in their feelings.

Depending on which stage the individual is in, that "testing" is performed with tantrums, pushing the limits, sharp responses, or spikes in adrenaline or depression.

Starting from a pure dependence on emotions when we are babies we should, as time goes by, begin to connect our feelings to knowledge, experiences, and a greater use of reason as we face different stimuli.

In the inner universe of the new generations, different emotional needs take on an urgency status, according to the different phases, and that is why these diverse feelings are fully exposed. Some teachers sometimes lose sight of the fact that, although teenagers have adult bodies, emotionally they are not quite there adults yet. An example is when a retreat ends and they feel like they are in heaven, but the following weekend they've fallen in love with the wrong person. Their emotions can be very extreme, and that is why we cannot assume that they are in heaven when they have the right information or they get excited with spiritual stimuli, nor believe that they've fallen into a bottomless pit, if after they manage what we consider an accomplishment they follow it up with a huge stumble.

Acceptance, regulation, and stability are the objectives to be achieved in our emotional development; our feelings will always be there, since they are also part of God's engineering.

SOCIAL

Each of us is wired for relationships, and it is through our interaction with other people that we interpret our own identity, vocation and destiny.

"Life's friends" are not a minor detail in the spiritual formation of people, and the best parents, teachers, leaders and pastors are intentional in facilitating and promoting the kind of positive relationships that new generations need.

Childhood is a stage of protection, where social contact is limited —albeit unconsciously—by the will of the parents, while in adolescence the family is giving up prominence to other contacts and places in which new generations unfold. In these new environments, new questions emerge, and different roles are being rehearsed in order to find one's own place.

The race for coexistence and adaptation runs along the social track. The main questions are: *"Who am I?" "Do I look good?" "Who do I want to be?" "What do others think of me?"* These are the issues at stake behind the relationships and the groups that are being formed. The acceptance of their peers is important and it can even be of great benefit for their development, although much of what comes with it is a source of discomfort and anxiety to adults. The truth is that acceptance and recognition by a group provides support to a growing individual who still feels unworthy of coping with adulthood.

Even conflicts with our childhood or adolescent peers present a great opportunity to mature, because when we reach adulthood we all will have to work with difficult people or in situations in which we disagree with others.

Pastors, parents, and Christian leaders should then know that the ways in which new generations learn to relate during each stage will determine mechanisms in their behavior, in their emotional responses and in their confidence to start new relationships and sustain them or change them as adults. This is not, and cannot become, a superfluous detail in our task of discipleship.

SPIRITUAL

Identity and purpose create an equation with no results unless the spiritual aspect is answered. All human beings have a spiritual area designed by God. Even the child or adolescent of the most agnostic or antireligious family questions himself about

IDENTITY AND PURPOSE CREATE AN EQUATION WITH NO RESULTS UNLESS THE SPIRITUAL ASPECT IS ANSWERED

his meaning. At some point they will be in their bed staring at the ceiling, wondering if there really isn't somebody beyond.

Identity, freedom, and truth are three key words for the new generations... and also for the Bible. When Jesus told some Jews, "If you hold to my teaching, you are really my disciples. Then you will know the truth, and the truth will set you free" (John 8:31–32), he was linking the searches that are a product of someone's path to maturity. The new identity in Christ that the born-again Christian obtains frees him from the bonds that deny spiritual life, and opens up the possibility of development also in this dimension.

The search for truth is nothing other than a search for God, because he is the Truth (John 14:6); the search for freedom is also nothing other than a search for God, because he is the Lord (Philippians 2 :11); and the search for identity is nothing more than a search for God, because he is the Creator (Isaiah 42:5).

EVEN THE CHILD OR ADOLESCENT OF THE MOST AGNOSTIC OR ANTIRELIGIOUS FAMILY QUESTIONS HIMSELF ABOUT HIS MEANING

> *The transition from adolescence to youth is also the transition from affiliative faith to personal faith. The former is the faith of the group, and parents are happy because their children tend to be heavily involved in the church group. The more activities their children participate in, the more satisfied parents feel. But affiliative faith is not valid for adult life. Young people have to decide what role they want faith to play in their life project. And parents and the church are fundamental pieces for a successful transition between one stage and another.*
>
> *- Felix*

HOLISTIC APPROACH

The development of each area stimulates the development of the others. When new generations develop spiritually they are more likely to be emotionally healthy, to be positive agents in social life, to feel secure in the development of their intellect, and also to find it easier to have a healthy balance.

Generational leadership proposes a holistic or complete approach not only because it looks beyond the spiritual dimension without isolating it from the other tracks of development, but also because it respects the different maturation phases of God's design and its psychosocial components in order to do a more precise pastoral job that optimizes the results we want and can obtain.

Chapter 6

SITUATIONAL LEADERSHIP

True leadership starts with love.

Glenn C. Stewart

Leadership is easy until it includes people.

Interrelationships have always been complex, but the speed at which connections change today, the flow of information that we access since childhood, and the "glamorization" by the media of certain dangerous behaviors, make leading the new generations a true challenge.

In the major universities of Europe it has become common to speak of a "VUCA" world. This term was created by the famous West Point military academy. This acronym refers to the fact that we live surrounded by a high index of volatility, uncertainty, complexity, and ambiguity.

"Leadership in a VUCA world" is precisely one of the subjects I teach at the university. The ability to unlearn in order to be able to relearn, flexibility, agility, and ability to adapt to a changing environment are essential competencies that every leader should intentionally cultivate and develop. And that, of course, also includes us, the Christian leaders.

- Felix

LEADERS MUST ASK OURSELVES IF WHAT WE DO CONTINUES TO MAKE SENSE IN A RAPIDLY CHANGING ENVIRONMENT

But there is good news hidden in the challenges! Even though they may try to make us believe that it is not so, as preadolescents who do not want us to discover that they are in love, the new generations desire to be led. They desire a leadership that is transparent, close, less dogmatic and more relational, where there are shared visions and agility in communication. Children admire preteens, and preteens admire teenagers, while these in turn look with esteem at university students. This instinctive memory was designed by God, and both in the church and in the family we must learn to manage with wisdom the possibilities that this truth presents. Herein also lies the beauty of the vision of generational leadership.

The respected author Peter Drucker had already said several decades ago, "An organization must periodically challenge each product, service, policy and distribution channel to avoid being held hostage by the circumstances." If this statement was true more than thirty years ago, it is even more urgent today. Leaders must ask ourselves if what we do continues to make sense in a rapidly changing environment. Inertia is so dangerous that it can kill us.

If we already understand clearly that the great goal in the spiritual formation of the new generations can be summed up in accompanying each child, preadolescent, adolescent and youth toward maturity in Christ (Colossians 1:28), the next step is to discern how to lead them, taking into account their different stages of maturity, since obviously the way to attract, involve and mobilize a child or a teenager will not be the same, even if at age seven, twelve, or twenty-three there may be common interests and they may need intergenerational relationships.

The time has come to begin to understand that there are different styles of leadership, and that one is not necessarily better than another. The appropriate style depends on context. Circumstances and maturity will determine which will be the best style.

Are you surprised by my statement? Well, I was surprised at how, in our churches, the idea that there is only one "superstyle" of effective leadership was anchored, and that is why in this chapter I want us to break this legend together.

PREDISPOSITION LEVELS

Let's start by analyzing the leadership styles in light of the maturity of those we lead. For this, I invite you to call the level of maturity the "predisposition level."

We cannot expect a child to express himself as an adult, nor pretend to achieve an optimal result when trying to influence him with the same tactics with which we influence a university student. Three widely recognized authors within the business administration environment, Hersey, Blanchard and Johnson, defined "predisposition" as "the extent to which a follower demonstrates the ability and desire to complete a specific task."[1]

In a broad sense, the desired task in the case of spiritual formation can be identified as the assimilation of the purposes described in chapter four as lifelong habits. But in this chapter I want to also consider the topic of the church programs.

According to the model proposed by these authors, the main components of predisposition are skill and disposition, and bringing their analysis to our discussion, let's also add maturity to the picture.

I will ask you to have patience now, since here we are going to get a little technical, but I really want to share these schemes because they help us complete the diagram that we described in the strategic vision in chapter 3. I promise you that by following these ideas with

---

1   Hersey, Blanchard y Johnson. *Management of Organizational Behavior - Leading Human Resources.* 9th Ed. Upper Saddle River, NJ: Pearson Prentice Hall; (2008).

precision you will find that they can have a powerful impact on your task.

LEVELS OF PREDISPOSITION TO PARTICIPATION

Predisposition levels

P1 Low	P2 Moderate	P3 Unstable	P4 High
Not willing	Willing	Not willing	Willing
Not able	Not able	Able	Able
Children	Preadolescents	Adolescents	Young adults

PREDISPOSITION #1: CHILDREN

We must convince children that Jesus is billions of times better than anyone or anything else in the universe. They can learn stories about the character of Christ, behavior that is desirable and undesirable, and the importance of Christian priorities, even though in contrast to the purposes that are evidence of spiritual maturity, they will have a hard time embracing the heart of the purposes as habits of the soul and as the internal motor of their behaviors. And that's fine. The level of disposition should not be confused with repeating behaviors, because most children at this phase have no problems imitating what they see. The disposition to which we refer is an internal reality toward the heart of what we teach them.

PREDISPOSITION #2: PREADOLESCENTS

Now there is a more personal interest, not only in the behavior but in the "why" of the behavior. Specific and creative tasks begin to generate greater disposition, especially in those who receive positive affirmation from their leaders. As far as ability, in general terms—although they may surprise us sometimes—preadolescents will still not be experienced enough to carry out any tasks that require individual initiative.

PREDISPOSITION #3: ADOLESCENTS

Adolescents can be considered skilled at beginning to demonstrate the purposes in their own initiatives. They have accumulated enough experience and can now visualize external tasks with an internal connection in a clear and individual way. The curious thing about this stage is that it usually lowers their level of disposition. There are two reasons for this: on the one hand, they now depend a lot on their peer group, and on the other hand, they now are the ones who begin to be in charge of their tasks, and they are expected to perform them well.

From the church's perspective, at this age they cease to be recipients and become creators of the processes, and they begin to demand prominence. Being closer to the leaders gives adolescents the opportunity to be in charge of achieving the purposes and executing the tasks. Of course, being still immature when it comes to dealing with their fundamental needs, adolescents often encounter difficulties in their interpersonal relationships. Platonic crushes and family crises related to limits will arise, and this will interfere with their confidence to gain more responsibilities.

PREDISPOSITION #4: YOUNG ADULTS

The purposes can and should be developed and demonstrated autonomously. Young people make executive decisions with normalcy, and may be interested in the ministry's productivity if they are sufficiently stimulated. (It is a sign of adulthood to remain productive without continuous external stimuli.) Youth take over tasks motivated by group recognition, or they exclude themselves from the church because they now have a personal agenda that does not depend on their parents.

From the perspective of the church, they may have disposition if their personal interests are met, if they have the ability, and if their fundamental needs are sufficiently dealt with, enabling them to concentrate on productivity.

In summary:

P1. Demands a strong pedagogy concrete enough to take advantage of the high data retention that exists at this stage. Needs to see.

P2. Demands involvement and needs to know what is behind the information. Needs to understand.

P3. Demands belonging and an external and energized expression of internal commitments. Needs to believe.

P4. Demands freedom. Is able to assimilate the purposes without strong relational behavior on the part of the leaders and without relying on the level of attraction of the program. Needs confidence.

LEADERSHIP STYLES

I enjoy exploring the classic books that became the basis for theories that later created new vocabularies. Books that, after all, are the foundations of what comes next. That's the case with Robert R. Blake and Jane Mouton's book titled *The Managerial Grid*, which influenced the classical management schools and was the basis for the marketing and leadership revolution that came later. In this book, Blake and Mouton proposed an ideal leadership style, which reinforced the old myth that when it came to leading, there was one superstyle. According to their grid, there are two fundamental variables in the execution of influence:

1. Concern for *people*

2. Concern for *production*

Let's recall the diagram described in chapter 3. These variables fulfill the same function as the constants of relationships and programs, and that is why it is important to pay attention to what Blake and Mouton said. Their thesis is that the level of results in an organization depends on leaders placing a high interest in close relationships, and also a high interest in production (or in the activities and programs). Sounds good, right?

At first glance it appears that it does, and clearly its proposal is the standardized premise about leadership in most Western churches, since it is the traditional position of those who have been involved in the training of Christian leaders. But Blake and Mouton forgot to analyze the variable of the maturity of the leaders, or the impact of large-scale leadership when working in organizations that have multiplied in numbers.

That's why the additions of authors Hersey, Blanchard and Johnson, which we mentioned earlier, are so vital. Studying their ideas broadened my vision. These authors proposed that there is no such thing as an ideal style to achieve the desired performance. What we have is different styles that are productive in different situations. In other words, the best leadership is the one that "learns" to adapt its style to different situations.Hersey, Blanchard and Johnson identified four leadership styles:

- **Style 1** – Highly autocratic leadership. (**S1**)
  - Someone who gives orders.
  - Places a lot of emphasis on programs, activities and results.
  - Close relationships are not a priority.
  - Makes most decisions.
  - Gives precise instructions.
  - Closely supervises results.
  - Sets goals for the entire organization.
  - Defines the roles of others.

- **Style 2** – Highly autocratic and highly relational leadership. (**S2**)
  - Perceived as someone who inspires and persuades.
  - A lot of emphasis on programs, activities and results.
  - Cares about close relationships.
  - Persuades others to follow his decisions.
  - Gives open instructions, giving the opportunity to his followers to add their own criteria.
  - Inspires others to follow their own goals.
  - Explains the roles of others, pointing out their importance.

- **Style 3** – Highly relational leadership. (**S3**)
  - Gives priority to relationships and puts programs and activities in the background.
  - Is perceived as someone who shares.
  - Low participation in programs, activities and results.
  - Very careful to keep harmony in a group.
  - Strives for consensus in decisions.
  - Decisions are made as a group.
  - Reaches an agreement regarding the instructions.
  - Asks others what their goals are.
  - Subordinates establish their own roles.

- **Style 4** – Minimally autocratic and relational leadership. (**S4**)
  - In its positive facet is perceived as someone who delegates and allows others to be and do.
  - Low participation in programs and activities.
  - Little investment in close relationships.
  - Lets everyone make their own decisions.
  - Limits himself to indicate the expected final result.
  - Subordinates establish their own roles.

Perhaps this image will help you understand it better.

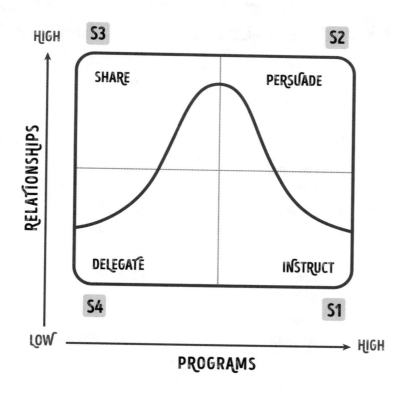

STYLES, RELATIONS AND PROGRAMS

The great idea that emerges from these concepts is that there are different styles that can be effective according to different ages and different ministerial situations. Effective leaders have what in some sports we call, in Spanish, *cintura* (waist), meaning that they are able to read and change the play while running in the direction of the goal. Each style can be used correctly or incorrectly based on the situational needs required to order, persuade, share or delegate, as shown in the following table:

	POSITIVE	NEGATIVE
S1	Define Guide Direct Set	Demands Controls Attacks Limits
S2	Persuade Sell Inspire Explain	Manipulates Uses Deceives Justifies
S3	Share Encourage Accompany Respect	Fear Buy Overprotect Looks good with everyone
S4	Delegate Observe Assign Give freedom	Quits Avoids Dodges Careless

I've had the privilege of working with a large number of leaders with different leadership styles in various contexts, and my experience confirms the premise of situational leadership: **there is not just one way to lead well**.

There is not just one mold.

There is not a superstyle.

There is not a recipe that always works.

Effective generational leaders are not all athletic men who play the guitar. The best teachers of children and preadolescents are not all pleasant women with high-pitched voices. The best pastors are not all ultraefficient managers who lead a congregation as if it were a multinational corporation.

GENERATIONAL VISION, STYLES AND LEVELS OF PREDISPOSITION

The following figure represents the movement of the different styles in relation to the constants of the ministry and the levels of predisposition.

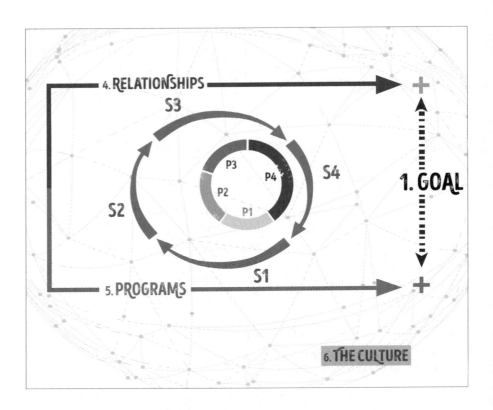

S1

This is the ideal style to command the necessary actions that facilitate practical objectives. Leaders who use this style put a lot of emphasis on the program and the measurable objectives. Regarding the new generations, this style usually works best when the followers are P1. For P1, creativity and program structure are fundamental. There are always affective children who need an emotional connection, but they do not demand close mentoring to join the church program. P1 needs the leaders to provide the initiative, direction, parameters and limits. S1 also works very well when you have to generate a strategic plan, such as when starting a new organization or at the beginning of a new ministry or complex activity. S1 is the style of leadership that achieves external results with greatest ease.

S2

They are the great motivators. It is ideal for a P2 preadolescent with the willingness to participate but without the ability and maturity to perform autonomously at an ideal level. S2 is excellent for taking members of a ministry to a higher level of maturity, because it knows how to do it by being highly programmatic and highly relational.

S3

They are democratic. Consensus and balance are two important words for them. This style is not fascinated by the "mega," but its emphasis is on relationships. While they are not always the most popular in the church in general, it is easy to see S3 leaders saying that numbers are not important to them, or listen to them explain how they are convinced that theirs is the true spiritual leadership. Although it seems counterintuitive, S3 is ideal for P3 adolescents, members who have the ability to execute but who need strong emotional support to get going. P3 needs to feel respected to be able to execute at their level of ability, and this leadership style gives them the necessary support. Of course, always remembering that what's important is the growth of these adolescents, rather than the lights at the massive conference.

S4

This is the style that usually works best with P4. The P4 youth have had enough opportunities to practice, they feel confident about being able to achieve the results, and they have the maturity necessary to function autonomously. The leader does not need to tell them every-thing they have to do, or persuade them to work toward the purposes. Nor do they need to agree with the leader on everything regarding the procedures. The P4 youth are the new leaders within a healthy organi-zation, and they are the ones who work the relationships and programs

THE NEW GENERATIONS NEED LEADERS WHO CAN DISCERN THEIR NEEDS AND LEARNING STYLES

toward the purposes. When S4 works well, the leader delegates without abandoning, and gives greater freedom for young people to shape strategies. Although it may seem at first glance that he has lost the reins, his impact is powerful in exercising the ministry of "being present," legitimizing the works of those he leads.

The new generations need leaders who can discern their needs and learning styles, and who know how to alternate leadership styles according to the circumstances.

We have to leave behind the machista myths that tell us we always need a super general director to make things work, or that the most spiritual ministries are the ones that spend more time with people without paying attention to the programs.

> This whole chapter fascinates me and it made me laugh to think that we can also add the differences in leadership styles between men and women. For example, when men are upset with a situation in the ministry they tend to evade it or withdraw. They usually look for some time alone to go for a walk, a drive or a run. It is their cave. Women, on the other hand, need to talk, share, feel understood and talk a little more. This is part of how men and women are wired, and it would be very naive to believe that one of these tendencies is better or worse than the other.
>
> *-Kara*

The outstanding leaders we urgently need are all-terrain people, who learn to adapt to different circumstances and vary their leadership styles according to the situation. They are focused on the goal and love people, even if they are not necessarily always extroverted and outgoing.

Now let's think about ourselves. If, when you saw the descriptions, you identified a tendency in your leadership style and said, "This is me," I encourage you not to stay there, even if you have already been in ministry for many years. We all can and must change.

Be transformed by the renewal of your mind (Romans 12:2).

All Christians, including leaders, are continuously in the process of growing, and this is one of the most beautiful facets of developing our talents. Although it may be difficult, we can move past our own nature and develop new talents or skills that did not seem to be part of our innate strengths.

> *That's a powerful point, and different from some of the ideas about leadership that have settled in the heart of the church, just because we assumed that certain gurus of modern American leadership had always been right.*
>
> *Also, in his book* Lead Like Jesus, *Ken Blanchard, a committed follower of Christ, helps us to understand that the Master was a situational leader who adapted his leadership style to people and circumstances, and was comfortable using all of the leadership styles. Jesus was clearly directive at the beginning of his ministry, and yet he was delegating completely at the end, as the great commission shows.*
>
> *- Felix*

In the @institutoE625 we offer a foundational course on leadership styles that can help you better identify your recurring style and analyze how you can learn to use other styles when necessary.

A CASCADING TEAM

What comes to light when talking about the different styles and trends is that it is impossible to achieve the greatest impact in the church if we only have one person in charge of everything, especially if the goal is discipleship and not just to have all the seats filled.

> I completely agree, Lucas! Reality is increasingly complex, and there is no one leader in the world, no matter how well prepared, who can have the ability to encompass, process and understand all aspects or facets of reality. We need work teams that provide complementary visions, which will allow us to have a broader and more accurate picture of reality.
>
> *- Felix*

WE NEED MULTIDISCIPLINARY TEAMS IN EACH OF THE AREAS OF THE GENERATIONAL PASTORAL WORK

We need multidisciplinary teams in each of the areas of the generational pastoral work.

We need to recruit more volunteers for the children's ministry, develop the preadolescent ministry, accommodate the adolescents, and not lose the university-aged youth, especially considering all the pressures they are now encountering in their new adult world.

The church must learn to involve the parents.

Parents must learn to rely on the church.

We need to take advantage of the possibility of generating a cascade of leadership, involving preadolescents as participants in the children's ministry, adolescents in the preadolescent ministry, and university-aged youth in the adolescent ministry, while university students find married couples that model a mature adulthood and help them make the right decisions.

Think about it for a moment. Why do so many university students today not want to get married, instead intending to perpetuate their adolescence until they are thirty years old? Isn't it because they don't have enough married adults around to cause them to experience a "holy envy" and make them want to be married and reach adulthood?

In addition, those who lead the new generations must break the fragmentation we inherited and learn to count on each other no matter what our official role is.

And we should look outside of the confines of Christian influence, and keep an eye on what happens at schools or universities where the new generations deal with other influences.

Look again at the basic diagram of the vision of generational discipleship.

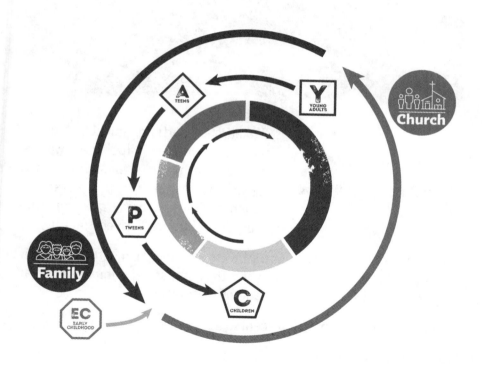

The ideal picture for a church that reaches the new generations is complete when in the picture we have leaders whose tendencies cover the four styles, and we have at least one married couple with each stage modeling situational leadership. As the writer of Ecclesiastes said, "Two are better than one, because they have a good return for their labor" (Ecclesiastes 4:9).

> Today many adolescent and youth ministries, especially in the United States, promote building relationships between peers of their same age. But while peer relationships are crucial, and it is very good that they have them, many studies highlight that intergenerational relationships are even more powerful in facilitating spiritual maturation and nurturing a vibrant faith. Therefore, reimagining the ministry with more adults involved in the leadership of new generations and activating those new generations in discipleship of those who follow them is no doubt a powerful vision.
>
> *- Kara*

GENUINE DISCIPLESHIP SPACES HAVE NO WALLS

We all need partners in meeting goals, copilots who can pilot when we are tired. That is why communion is a means to reach our full potential, when facing the great goal and the purposes that are derived from it.

The cascade of influence is God's invention, and we must take advantage of it. Children learn best when they can see the impact of what they've learned in their next stage of maturation.

Children want to be preadolescents.

Preadolescents want to be adolescents.

Adolescents dream of being young adults.

And university-aged youth need mature adults who model for them the abundant life of which Jesus spoke (John 10:10).

Genuine discipleship spaces have no walls. They are multipurpose classrooms that cannot be reduced to a church building or a family dinner. These spaces are valuable and decisive, but there is so much more to explore.

Max Depree wrote that true leadership never ends with words. And long before he wrote it, the one who modeled that idea was our great teacher, Jesus of Nazareth. He was the best of all leaders, and a clear example of someone who used different tactics according to different situations. We could learn so much from him.

Chapter 7

THE NECESSARY PLAN

*He who loves practice without theory is like the sailor who
boards ship without a rudder and compass and
never knows where he may cast.*

Leonardo da Vinci

Few things discourage me more than seeing churches go out of business. I had never seen one, until I arrived from Argentina to study in the United States. The first one I found was in California. It looked abandoned, and had a "for sale" sign out front. The first thing I thought was that the congregation must have moved to a bigger place, but since the church was close to where I lived, one day I asked some pastors who were my friends and lived in the area about it. How great was my disappointment when they told me that the congregation had closed its doors because its members had aged and were so few that they could no longer pay the taxes or keep up the property.

How does a church go out of business?

Unfortunately, since that first encounter with a closed local church, I have known about many others that also went out of business in various parts of the world. They all have different stories, but there are, however, two common denominators: they never thought it would happen to them, and they were not effective in working with the new generations.

When I entered the University of Buenos Aires to study law, the Lord gave me, I must say "miraculously," the opportunity to teach tennis at preschools. I say miraculously because, although I knew the rules and some technique, I'm still terrible at that sport. I remember the day I started teaching at a small kindergarten in the northern area of the city, in a neighborhood where everyone lives in apartment buildings. The school did not have a sports facility, so we would take the four- and five-year-old little ones to tennis courts that were some distance away.

WE MUST NEVER CHANGE THE SACREDNESS OF THE GOSPEL, BUT WE MUST INNOVATE IN PERIPHERAL ISSUES

I remember that first class. Once we got comfortable, the first thing I told my little students was to go ahead and run freely wherever they wanted. I thought that they were going to enjoy that, and that they would go running all over the place, but to my surprise, I noticed that they began to go around in circles in a very small area, and some even circled around almost without moving from their place. I repeated to them that they could run freely, and I remember that some began to circle around me. Then I told them to run to the net, or to the wall, and it was only then that they started to run without going in circles.

It got me thinking.

These were children who lived in vertical buildings, and they had learned to run inside small rooms. They were so used to running in those small spaces that, when given a new freedom, they didn't know how to do something different.

Doesn't it remind you a little bit of the church?

We need to renew our programs. We need to learn that change is not the enemy! Of course we must never change the sacredness of the gospel, but we must innovate in peripheral issues.

The combination of musical notes, the aesthetics, whether or not we raise our hands, what time the meeting starts, how we sit, how we decorate the stage, on what days we schedule the youth meeting, and the format of the Bible school, or whatever we call it, those are not doctrine. They are just traditions and strategies.

Jesus calls the church to raise new generations that can live the great commandment and the great commission, but does not specify precisely "how" we are supposed to

WE NEED AN ORGANIC PLAN THAT CAN CONTINUALLY BE ADJUSTED TO THE NEEDS OF AN AREA, A SOCIAL TYPE, AND A SPECIFIC GENERATION

carry it out. Why? Because the methods are never sacred! If we look closely at the Bible, we find Jesus saying what needs to be achieved, but not saying too much about how to achieve it. We even see him, for example, always using different ways to heal the blind. Why? Because the great Master knew that many earthlings are fascinated by magic formulas, and he was deliberately emphasizing that the method is not sacred.

> *Leadership experts assert that in a world as complex as the one we live in, what is required is complete unity in the purpose to be achieved, and complete freedom in the means to achieve it.*
>
> **- Felix**

The apostle Paul did not add much about the forms and methodologies that the church should use. In 1 Corinthians he says that everyone's gifts should be used, because they have been given by the Spirit, and that it should be done in an orderly manner (1 Corinthians 12 and 14). Then he writes to Titus and Timothy about what the leaders' requirements are (Titus 1 and 1 Timothy 3), but he doesn't add much more about how church programming should be carried out. Why? Because while there are sacred purposes, there are no sacred methodologies. The Bible does not change, and God does not change, but each generation of the church must find how to be effective in fulfilling the purposes in their own temporal and spatial context.

That is why we need an organic plan that can continually be adjusted to the needs of an area, a social type, and a specific generation.

Jesus puts us on the court and invites us to run freely. How about we stop running in small circles?

WE CANNOT ALLOW OURSELVES TO BE ANESTHETIZED BY THE SEDUCTIVE CARESSES OF OUR TRADITIONS

Ninety percent of the churches I know have a youth meeting that is an exact copy of the Sunday adult service, except for being on a different day of the week and with younger people. Everyone is sitting down looking at the back of the neck of the person in front of them. They stand to sing. They sit. They stand to sing. They say "hello" to the person next to them. They sit down again without talking about what's happening. (Never mind asking questions, because that would be too much rebellion in some places.) The same thing happens in the children's ministry, except that, since we've already figured out that during the sermon it's very difficult for them to pay attention, we prefer to play a movie for them.

This basic church service format of today was inherited from the Catholic Church of the Middle Ages, because although the Catholic worship focuses on the Eucharist and the evangelical on preaching, the expectation regarding the participation of the attendees is almost the same. The Protestant Reformation, with Luther and Calvin, changed our theological understanding, but did not change much of the format of the meetings. The charismatic reform, from Wesley, through the Azusa Street revival where Pentecostalism was officially born, and all the way to the music renewal movements, all fundamentally changed the ways Christians express themselves but, although they added more spontaneity and renewed aesthetics and harmonies, they did not change the basic format of the church services.

Let's make it clear: The great commission does not say "go and have meetings," much less tell us exactly how we should sit or how long the meetings should last. We cannot allow ourselves to be anesthetized by the seductive caresses of our traditions. And, again, I am not speaking here of intentions. I am speaking of being courageous enough to ask ourselves the important questions, and of being willing to pay the price for changing the paradigms.

What tends to catch us stealthily is the subtle and cowardly sin of inertia. We remain comfortable doing what we have always done, what we already know, and what does not arouse the criticisms or suspicions of bleacher Christians, who are always ready to criticize those who walk the runways of a bold ministry.

What then should we do? I say again that there are no magic formulas, and yet there are some connections.

TWO SACRED CONNECTIONS

Programming effectively does not come down to doing some isolated superactivities. We must establish a plan, draw up a strategy, and implement a schedule. That is why the following connections, although they may be useful for individual activities, are mostly aimed at a general annual planning.

A balanced, biblical, and effective strategic plan always makes two connections:

> **Connection #1. With Christ's purposes for the church**
>
> **Connection #2. With God's integral design**

CONNECTION #1: WITH CHRIST'S PURPOSES FOR THE CHURCH

It seems obvious, right? But it's not.

In many churches, an exorbitant amount of effort is spent with the sole purpose of filling up the auditorium; to do better than the congregation or the denomination next door by booking the latest star singer, preacher or celebrity because no one else in the city can book them; having the largest building in the area—out of pride—or doing what is "in vogue" because that is what "moves people." All of this instead of meditating conscientiously about how to achieve God's purposes.

Of course, we rarely will confess to doing something like that. It is always someone else who's doing it; it is never us. You may remember that in a previous chapter we said that when there are no clear purposes there are usually selfish goals. And there is always a reason why we do things, even if we try to hide it! That is why it is so crucial to focus our eyes toward the purposes we are pursuing, and to be honest in asking ourselves: Are we really achieving what Jesus wants us to achieve, or are we simply fulfilling our own agenda?

> *Certainly having a vision is crucial, although it should be noted that not all churches and leaders understand the same thing when we say vision, and that is why I like the clarity that Scott Cormode brought to the topic when he defined "vision" as "shared stories that bring hope." This definition offers three aspects of a regenerative vision: shared, stories, hope. The first aspect implies that the vision does not arise from the mind of a single isolated person. It is created by the different stories that are intertwined. And the third aspect is a future hope anchored in the good news about Jesus for the whole world. When the vision is nurtured in this way, rather than being created by a single person, there are many more guarantees that it will be the right plan with the right motivations and without those typical selfish goals that Lucas mentions.*
>
> *-Kara*

Leadership without direction, set up only to reach "great milestones" or to maintain those that have already been reached, always depends on sporadic activities to ignite the enthusiasm of the new generations. A special night of worship with some well-known musicians, a retreat, or a theater play with many children involved certainly lifts the spirits and attracts everyone's attention. But to build a ministry that facilitates genuine maturation, it is necessary that the purposes be the main reason why we do all that is done, and there must be something more than a few "superevents" scattered throughout the year. Behind each activity there must be a clear motivation that transcends it. Why are we having a retreat? What is the reason for a concert? And, more importantly, how is each specific event connected with the priorities of this congregation at this precise moment in its history?

> I absolutely agree! In my book Roots: Pastoral Youth in Depth I expressed the opinion that every ministry should be based on processes and not on events. The latter are important and necessary, but only as long as they are part of the process and contribute to its development. Otherwise, events become ends in themselves, instead of means to achieve a higher purpose. That is why, before planning an event, we must ask ourselves: What process is this a part of? What contribution does the event make to the process?
>
> - **Felix**

We cannot merely use purposes as excuses to organize certain activities without making them the real motivation. This becomes reflected in the results. For example, we may say that an activity is "evangelistic," but we only advertise it in other churches, with evangelical language and evangelical personalities, and without an effective mobilization to attract those who do not know Jesus. And to be clear: I don't think there is anything wrong with organizing concerts or having bands that are only for Christians, or in planning large events where we Christians as a community enjoy God's word. This is all wonderful! What I am saying is that we have to be honest in asking ourselves why we do it and for whom. This is essential to be able to evaluate if what we are planning to do is really the right strategy to achieve what we intend to achieve.

If I say that I want to promote a serious and deep reflection about leadership, will it be better to bring the most popular musician on the social networks, or will it be better to bring an experienced leader, who knows a lot about leadership and has a proven record of having successfully led in the past?

EFFECTIVE LEADERSHIP DRAWS PRAGMATIC PLANS TO ACHIEVE ITS PURPOSES EFFECTIVELY

Effective leadership draws pragmatic plans to achieve its purposes effectively, and always questions whether what has traditionally been done, or what everyone else is doing, really achieves what it wants to achieve.

Now, perhaps all of this fits the "activist" churches, but at the other extreme we also have many churches that focus on keeping the traditions so as to not "abandon the old path," using the excuse that they are doing it to protect "the sound doctrine." But which biblical doctrine are they really protecting? And what exactly is the old path? Obviously, at least for chronological reasons, when the Bible speaks of "the old path" or "the right way" in Jeremiah 6, we cannot think that it is referring to the traditions that European missionaries imported into America two centuries ago. The old path refers to the values that God always had, which must find an active application among us today.

> I can hardly agree more with Lucas. It is increasingly clear to me that confronting the present with methods from the past can lead to mortgaging the future.
>
> **- Felix**

The wake-up call is clear: We cannot claim to lead the new millennium generation to the fulfillment of Christ's purposes with the methodologies of the last century, nor can we continue to depend on sporadic activities without having the correct purposes in mind, just because they are the ones that attract more people... from other churches. In other words, we need programming that creates processes consistent with what we believe we should achieve.

CONNECTION #2: WITH GOD'S INTEGRAL DESIGN

As soon as his ministry began, Jesus announced, "The Spirit of the Lord is on me, because he has anointed me to proclaim good news to the poor. He has sent me to proclaim freedom for the prisoners and recovery of sight for the blind, to set the oppressed free, to proclaim the year of the Lord's favor" (Luke 4:18–19). As you can see, Jesus was connecting with the five tracks of development. Some theologians call this "holistic ministry," understanding that it includes the possibility, or the demand, to affect human life in all its dimensions.

Let us then consider together these five tracks.

THE PHYSICAL TRACK

How do we influence the physical body from the church's perspective? Well, for starters, how about if we develop a better relationship with sports? Sports help the ministry, mainly in two ways. First, sports are healthy. They are good for the temple of the Holy Spirit. Today many of our urban children and adolescents spend too much time locked up in their homes and at school. So what do we do? We tend to also lock them up in the church building. It's true that in many communities there are sports available provided by schools, but this is not the case in every city, nor can we assume that it is true in the life of each of our students. Our proposal is not to try to compete with what other institutions are offering, but rather to be attentive to the needs of our community, being sensitive to the fact that, if they are spending too much time in front of the different screens that modern technology offers them, it will be important to provide them with an option that will help them in their physical development.

The second valuable aspect of sports for the new-generation ministries is that they provide us an extraordinary opportunity to attract to the church those who otherwise would not be attracted by more traditional activities. A wise mixture of sports with evangelism is powerful. Today there are many ministries that combine sports and evangelism, with excellent results, and this strategy can be perfect for the local church. Leagues, tournaments and challenges are excellent tools to attract the new generations to the church.

The odd thing is that many congregations already have sports activities, especially for the older youth, but they are not intentional activities that are considered part of the church's plan. There's often an idea like, "On Tuesdays we meet with our friends from the church to play soccer," but it's not really considered a church activity. Are we sure that it is not?

Obviously I am not referring to just a soccer or basketball match here and there. With wise planning, there is truly a huge variety of physical activities that can be practiced and promoted by the church. We can also offer classes in sex education, nutrition and healthy eating habits, and rest cycles conducive to study. All these are subjects that the church can teach children, assisting them with their physical development in a positive way.

THE INTELLECTUAL TRACK

The well-known phrase "To believe is also to think," which British John Stott popularized, must constantly ring in the ears of those who work with the new generations. For many leaders and pastors, the biggest challenge with their group of adolescents, for example, is their youngsters' persistent attempts to question everything and ask "difficult" questions. I am surprised to find teachers who feel they are successful because their students never question them. If your adolescents never ask you tough questions and only speak in an "evangelical" dialect, something is not right. As we discussed above, preadolescents and adolescents begin to explore abstract thinking, and continue to develop through critical thinking. This process has its highest peaks at the beginning of adolescence and at the end, when

GOOD TEACHERS ENCOURAGE NEW GENERATIONS TO THINK, CRITICIZE, EVALUATE AND CONSIDER DIFFERENT OPTIONS IN THEIR SEARCH FOR THE TRUTH they arrive at the university and encounter an environment that causes them to question what they believe. Moreover, as we will develop more later, for this particular generation the indifference and social disenchantment caused by so many economic and political crises are two real challenges, and that is why it is so necessary to help them understand the truth, in order to give them hope.

Prensky, whom I already mentioned several times, says that our teaching to the new generations must be based on powerful questions that may provoke them to contemplate and think. We often give them answers to questions that do not concern or worry them, while we stop answering those questions that are important and urgent for them. That is why Prensky invites us—and I think he is absolutely right—to go one step further, not only by answering their questions, but by asking them questions that generate learning processes through reflection.

- Felix

The program for the new generations must allow times when critical thinking is encouraged rather than discouraged. Since childhood, the development of our convictions is manifested through questioning, and good leaders and teachers know how to help new generations to think, criticize, evaluate and consider different options in their search for the truth, based on the phase in which they are living.

THE EMOTIONAL TRACK:

Earlier we mentioned that the objectives to achieve in people's emotional development are stability, acceptance and regulation. In recent years, society has caused disenchantment and chronic anxiety, and this in turn has fueled feelings of dissatisfaction, indifference, dispersion and even depression in the hearts of the new generations. In a generation of digital natives, the instant pursuit of pleasure, driven by the media and facilitated by electronic devices, can interfere with the development of emotional maturity. The

ONLY A CENTURY AGO, THERE WAS NO SUCH THING AS AN ENTERTAINMENT INDUSTRY

entertainment industry looks to provoke ever stronger and stronger sensations and has an arsenal that it never had before. In fact, only a century ago, there was no such thing as an entertainment industry. Today our children's environment in major cities includes amusement parks with roller coasters that feature drops that previously seemed impossible. Music is omnipresent, virtual reality creates images that re-create the impossible, 3D movies are already the norm, the visual effects in concerts are almost as important as the music. Telephones are practically an extension of the body. Pornography is part of almost all publicity, advertisements, magazines and television programs, and is filtered even into the ads for the most harmless of applications. So much stimulus is difficult to control for someone who is in the process of maturation. And even more so when they believe that their value depends on what they do or what they have, and that acceptance depends on who they spend time with and who likes them on social media.

In the midst of so much advertisement appealing to immaturity and encouraging decisions based on feelings and impulses, it becomes complicated to develop into strong individuals, with a defined identity and strong inner convictions. That is why parents must learn to take refuge in the church, and the church must learn to team up with parents to disciple together new generations of strong and competent individuals able to stand against the powerful winds of a world that continually confuses the senses.

For all these reasons it is so vital that the program for the new generations must contemplate the organization of activities and the creation of teaching curricula where acceptance and unconditional love are a fundamental pillar, and refrain from creating sentimentalist atmospheres that only provide yet another environment for experiencing strong emotions without being regulated by the intellect.

Today, science has verified that children who experience unconditional love are statistically more likely to keep their faith on their road to adulthood, and although parental love is simply irreplaceable, when other adults sow that kind of love into the new generations, it fertilizes their volitional landscape, enabling them to make better decisions and facilitating their ability to heal from the wounds caused by a home without that kind of love.

-Kara

Programs that generate an environment of affection and acceptance will help the new generations to better process their emotions and to be able to control them, regulating their moods, impulses and sentimental reactions. A provocation and stimulation of the emotions that's immediately transferred to positive actions such as compassion and love can be positively channeled by facilitating activities that go beyond a weekly gathering. Experiences where they are able to express their feelings and put them into practice, such as by visiting either a juvenile correctional facility or sick children, or by confronting them with testimonials of extreme poverty or of bulimia and anorexia from some of those in a nearby rehab center. What's important is that visiting the needy, at an orphanage or nursing home, serves not only as an aid to the community, but also as a trigger of positive emotions that help the new generations bring out the best in themselves.

> Why don't we teach emotional intelligence in our churches? Human beings are eminently emotional. In Europe, education in the emotional intelligence field—meaning to understand our own emotions and how to regulate them, and to understand the emotions of others and how to regulate them—is increasingly considered fundamental to being able to have healthy and balanced lives and healthy interpersonal relationships with others. In addition, we know that when emotions become part of the learning process, this will be set deeper into our lives. The Bible has a lot to say about all these issues but, sadly, all too often it is absent from our educational processes.
>
> *- Felix*

THE SOCIAL TRACK

Earlier we explained that through this track we run the race of coexistence, adaptation, and exchanges, and the church must become the best place for each individual to socialize, because in it we must breathe unconditional love. As leaders we must facilitate this through our programs.

For example, in every group there is homogeneity and heterogeneity, and good programming can be used both to bring people closer to those who are more like them, and to help them relate to those who are different. Wouldn't this be of great assistance to facilitate a climate of inclusion in our cities? In the next chapter we will talk about the relational nuance of effective ministries, and we will better digest this principle, sharing ideas on how to integrate the different groups. For now, it is important to emphasize that we must program for the new generations to learn to relate better and make better friends, reconciling the social, racial and economic barriers that are the norm in the hyperpolarized environment that they already navigate.

When talking about this in different places, leaders have approached me to confess that they had never thought that this was part of their function, since they believed that their task was limited only to a

CHURCH MUST BECOME THE BEST PLACE FOR EACH INDIVIDUAL TO SOCIALIZE

weekly meeting or to the teaching of the word. But let us remember our purposes. Even God's word is a means to lead them to maturity, and not an end in itself. Communion and human relationships are avenues to help reach spiritual maturity, and it is absolutely impossible to separate the spiritual track from the social track. The impact that members of your ministry have among themselves is powerful, and if we exercise effective generational leadership we will learn to manage that impact and maximize it.

In fact, another very common mistake, especially in certain church circles, is to assume that new generations are always attracted to crowds. And, of course, we want more and more children, preadolescents, adolescents and youth to know God, but we must also notice that, if the new generations do not make friends in the church community, no matter how attractive the program is, they will have doubts about returning and persevering in becoming an important part of it. Although it is countercultural for some pastors and leaders over forty years old, drawing a crowd is no longer as attractive as it was a few decades ago. We live in a world that's moving more toward the personalized and communal, and that is why, although the attraction of large groups is undeniable at certain stages of life, the leader's mission is to make the experience feel small and personal.

If the new generations do not find companionship, personal advice, and a shoulder to cry on when needed, the lights, dynamic sermons and new decorations will not matter, and this explains why so many ministries that appear to be successful have so much turnover of people, and why so many people who get excited then make decisions that have nothing to do with what was taught.

At another extreme, there are leaders, especially in smaller environments, who have been caught up in the homogeneity of their closed group. The problem is that these groups have such strong codes that they scare away those who come from the outside. They are usually dominated by an elite group that the leader, teacher or pastor fears offending. The problem with this approach is that, by facilitating this marked homogeneity, they are limiting the opportunities to achieve other significant relationships, and they become paralyzed, limiting their role in the extension of the kingdom.

THE CHURCH MUST BE A PLACE OF REFUGE, WHERE THE NEW GENERATIONS CAN SOCIALIZE IN A POSITIVE WAY

What would be optimal? A program that combines a rotation of large groups with small groups, regardless of whether they are part of a large or a small church, because in both situations there are options to create positive environments. A strategy that includes diverse activities, where both recreation and personal interaction are important, will enrich the possibilities of the new generations as they go through the trial and error process in their relationships while they are content and safe in an environment created by mature leaders. The church must be a place of refuge, where the new generations can socialize in a positive way with their peers while compensating for or empowering family socialization.

> The concept of identity includes a personal dimension derived from how we see ourselves as opposed to others, but also a communal dimension derived from how we connect with others. Today's culture teaches the new generations to focus much more often on just responding to who they want to become, without considering the communal dimension, and that is why we become incredibly individualistic people. A rich and sustainable faith recognizes that as we walk alongside God's community, we also discover, by contrast, who we are.
>
> *- Kara*

THE SPIRITUAL TRACK

In the chapter about ecclesiology we made it clear that the purposes of Matthew 22:37–40 and Matthew 28:19–20 should be the aspiration of the ministry to the new generations when it comes to the spiritual track. This dimension is what is going to define inwardly the issue of becoming a complete person living the lifestyle of Christ.

The arenas of generational discipleship present the best opportunities to work on the values and behaviors expected of a Christian. From childhood to youth we are deeply sensitive to the possibility of adding role models to that identity that we are trying to define. That is why the spiritual disciplines must be part of the program, and not just topics in the classes. The volume of bad habits decreases when we increase the volume of good ones.

> **THE VOLUME OF BAD HABITS DECREASES WHEN WE INCREASE THE VOLUME OF GOOD ONES**

In most of our ministries we take lots of time to point out habits that are not recommended for believers, but more often than not we fail to offer alternatives, other than praying, reading the Bible and attending the church meetings. Fasting, service, individual worship, devotional life, simplicity, meditation, confession, silence, praise other than singing, communion, joy, retreats and other disciplines may become special experiences for the new generations if we can get them to experience them and notice their fruits from an early age.

Many years ago I wrote a small book for teens called *Don't Be a Dinosaur*, which dealt with how to make sure that our spiritual life does not die or dry out. In that book I describe some avenues in which adolescents can run without a speed limit toward experiencing God. Although it is a book that deals with classical spiritual disciplines, changing the language and calling them "avenues," the truth is that it immediately caught on and, to the surprise of those who told me that a book about disciplines would not work among teenagers, I soon found myself receiving messages from boys and girls who had begun to see these classic disciplines as an adventure.

One of the challenges for the programs when it comes to the spiritual aspect is the different degrees of spiritual maturity found in a group, as well as how it is expressed in the areas of growth. Believers' children know the stories, vocabulary, and memory verses, which makes newcomers feel like they "don't belong." A good program should deal with this difficulty in advance. Some alternatives are elective classes, short courses, inductive studies, group rotation or separate meetings. Later we will talk about the changes in our culture, and we will discuss how modernity has discredited the spiritual experience... with the good news that in recent times the "supra-sensory" experience has made a comeback.

The spiritual formation of the new generations is the basic objective of this whole discussion, and once we review our missionary paradigms, the time comes to adjust our programs.

NEW IDEAS, A NEW ARCHITECTURE

At the end of the book you will find an implementation guide to put into practice concrete steps that will help your local congregation to better respect each development area, and enable you to involve the whole church in creating a new missional architecture for the discipleship of the new generations, but let's start with where we are now.

Reggie Joiner, who for years led the family ministry at the influential North Point Church in Atlanta, highlights in his book *It's Just a Phase, So Don't Miss It* that we have 936 weeks from birth until we graduate from high school. In that book, he and his coauthor Kristen Ivy take a fabulous journey, condensing each phase from birth to graduation from the perspective of the most significant relationships, the realities, and the distinctive opportunities of each stage, and I think they hit the target by making it very clear that the discipleship work with the new generations is like a countdown.

The process of maturation is the great adventure of identity formation, and the church cannot miss this splendid opportunity to be a positive partner in defining that identity in as many children, preadolescents, adolescents, and youth as it can. That is

THE PROCESS OF MATURATION IS THE GREAT ADVENTURE OF IDENTITY FORMATION, AND THE CHURCH CANNOT MISS THIS SPLENDID OPPORTUNITY

our mission. We must mark the new generations with the signs of Jesus' disciples so they become people of integrity, maturity and fullness, chosen by God for the praise of his glorious grace (Ephesians 1:6). That's why we need ideas to hit the target much more often!

Certainly the process toward maturity is a journey in which we can enjoy the privilege of accompanying the new generations. Jesus approached the disciples who were on their way to Emmaus, and accompanied them in their spiritual condition, bringing the principles of the Word to their unique and specific reality. Experts in analyzing the new generations assert that boys and girls long for mentors to accompany them on their vital journey. What a great opportunity and what a great responsibility for us!

- Felix

The renewal of programs and activities should be done with elegance. Taking into account the ideas you will be reading below, think at first about how to add some salt to the things that your congregation is already doing, and you will be able to facilitate a renewed enthusiasm for your activities.

Carlos was a young pastor who attended one of the seminars we were offering in a Central American city. When he heard the story about my young tennis students and how they had ran in small circles, he thought, "That's what's happening to us!" At the end of my presentation he approached me and asked if we could talk for a few minutes.

I sat down with him and, as soon as we started talking, he began to release a stream of crazy ideas that he had thought about implementing in his congregation. The ideas seemed fantastic to me, and I encouraged him to keep up the good work. After a few months I met Carlos again at a convention and asked him how he was doing, and if he had already implemented any of those ideas. He looked at me with grief, and with his head down he told me that he had not been able to. As soon as he had returned from our seminar he had tried to turn around his ministry, doing everything he had not been able to do up to that time. In a few days he had half of his church against him, and to make matters worse, not even the youth had reacted to his ideas in the way he had expected.

CHANGING AT A 10 PERCENT PACE WORKS BEST IN 90 PERCENT OF THE CIRCUMSTANCES

What had happened? I had not been quick to warn him that changes should be made with elegance. Although his ideas were excellent, in his desire to change everything so suddenly he was unable to get others to understand what he was trying to do, and even his youth felt confused. We sat down again to talk. This time I shared a word that is very important in leadership: process. To implement changes takes time, and that is why changing everything so suddenly is not the wisest strategy.

In my own ministerial experience I learned that changing at a 10 percent pace works best in 90 percent of the circumstances. Sometimes we are looking forward so much to the wow factor, which is good to look for at times, that we lose sight of the fact that by making a small change to something we were already doing, we can generate a higher energy than with a completely new thing. That's because completely new things in general demand a period of adaptation or explanation, which can be avoided by simply renewing an aspect of something that everyone already knows.

Although this is a book of ministerial philosophy and not of specific ideas, let us be practical and go over a few ideas. But again, remember that for new ideas to work well, the renewal of programs and activities must be done as a process, introducing the changes little by little, over a period of well-planned transitions.

These are some "macro-ideas" that can facilitate many others.

SYNCHRONIZE THE CHURCH CALENDAR

In the Old Testament and even in the Gospels it is remarkable that the spiritual life of the people of God worked around a calendar of seven feasts.

Seven FEASTS. Yes, that word is in capital letters because it is obvious that, contrary to the vision we inherited from the last centuries, God has always cared about celebrations, and those celebrations were carefully put on a calendar so they could be anticipated and planned.

We must always plan, and we must plan celebrations. We must take advantage of the dates that are already important to the public by involving them in the planning and execution of special programs that take them into account.

Let's also consider those dates that are not in the general calendar, but are important to our specific audience, such as birthdays, graduations and the start of school. I remember vividly that when I was a teenager, many times I simply transported my body to a church meeting with the sole purpose of being in the right place where someone would then take me to a birthday party that was happening later. Why create a separation between the things that the new generations want to do, and that are good, and the church meeting? How about taking the meeting to the birthday party, or the birthday party to the meeting? Remember that it was our Lord who was criticized for spending time at parties, and he was also the one who compared the kingdom of heaven to a wedding party (Matthew 22:2–4).

A few years ago at the church where my wife and I pastored young people, we set up a big graduation party for all those who had finished high school and another one for those who had finished college, and although the first year there were only a few graduates, it was amazing the growth that was catapulted through these parties. We can organize an annual welcoming reception for those who come into the preadolescent ministry from the children's classes, and for the start and end of school, and we can be sensitive of the schedule of exams. These are all times to which we have to pay attention in our activities, when planning our themes. In fact, these graduation parties are the best device to facilitate a marked transition from one stage to another and a reception and graduation into a ministry.

If a group is small, we can include in the official calendar of the ministry a visit to a game of a young child who participates in a sport on his own, or a concert in which one of the preadolescents plays an instrument, because it is a good idea to take the rest of the young people to see them, or at the very least to make an open invitation so that some will go.

I remember one of my teenagers used to play volleyball in a municipal tournament, and her parents had told me that the final match was going to take place soon. I found out the date, and showed up at the match with some of her friends from the church. She didn't know that we were planning to go, and she was already playing when she realized that she had a group of "fans" in the stands who were chanting her name. Of course, she was a bit embarrassed (especially because I was there), but her reaction toward the youth ministry and toward me was never the same.

SURPRISE THEM

Too many children, preadolescents, adolescents and even young college students complain that the church is (let's say it together): B O R I N G! And one of the main reasons is that the activities are absolutely predictable. They know the order of things by memory, they know the favorite sayings of each leader, the scenery never changes, and the only real novelty is that on occasion the praise group learns a new song with a little jump to it.

We can all do better than that.

What if you were a preteen who arrives at the meeting, and without suspecting it you find a video of something you did during the week, that you didn't know someone had recorded? Did someone follow you? How did they get that? I have no doubt that you would think: I better come more often!

When I visit big camps and conferences for teenagers, I try to put myself in the shoes of the teenagers in order to talk to them. How can I get them to give me their attention to assimilate better what I am going

A PINCH OF SURPRISE CAN ENERGIZE A THOUSAND ACTIVITIES

to share with them? Thinking this way is the reason why I've said or done some things that later in social media videos have been taken out of context by some people or have been misinterpreted, precisely because others do not understand the context. That is one of the challenges today, when thousands of miles away, geographically or culturally, we try to understand what was said or done under other circumstances. But here we are talking about the ministry within the local church, and these are our children, preadolescents, adolescents or youth.

Think like they think.

You arrive at the meeting, and it turns out that a special guest is someone who sings one of your favorite songs and nobody had told you anything. Or they tell you to look under your seat and you find a number or a clue that gets you a prize. Or you are late and note that today there are more than twice as many young people at the meeting, and it's because your leaders arranged a united meeting with another church, because the theme of the night is unity, but it was all a surprise. Or you arrive early and you see that there is a huge cardboard curtain covering the door, from knee-high to the ceiling, and you see a sign that says: "He who humbles himself will be exalted... so today we will enter lowering our heads." Then you enter and it turns out that the theme of the night is to recognize who the Lord is and to humbly surrender to him.

What are your thoughts? Are you starting to want to attend this church? The possibilities are endless. A pinch of surprise can energize a thousand activities.

> Ernesto Yturralde wrote, "At school we learn the lesson and then we are tested; in life, we are first tested and then, only if we are attentive, we learn the lesson." Why don't we develop experiential learning in our churches? That's what Jesus did! He shared spiritual principles in the context of real and everyday life. Why do we insist on turning spiritual formation into an intellectual endeavor, directed exclusively at the brain and, too often, disconnected from real life? Imagine that you want to share with your teenagers or youth the biblical principle "Mercy I desire, and not sacrifice." Take them to one of the garbage dumps in the city, where children and adults live. Show them how these people live. Expose them to the reality of a fallen world. Then return to the church hall and reflect together on what that biblical principle means to you, and how you can apply it to those who live at the garbage dumps. Then, the following Saturday, go and put it into practice!
>
> **- Felix**

The element of surprise is very important to maintain attention and interest. Always doing the same thing is always tiresome, and it is very dangerous to create a sense of boredom in relation to the gospel. We have already lost too many children because of that.

Look at the stories about Jesus, as told in the Gospels, and you will notice that the disciples were going from surprise to surprise. First meeting: Jesus turns water into wine. Next time: Jesus asks them to feed a multitude, and when they look confused and don't know where to hide, he turns a couple of loaves and fishes into a massive feast.

Next meeting: The teacher enters by walking on water. Next time: He faces a demon-possessed man and sends the demons into a bunch of pigs. Another time: He resurrects! And even after that: He appears to them on the road, but doesn't let them know who he is. It is obvious that Jesus really enjoyed surprising his young people!

If you belong to an urban church, it is almost certain that among your ranks you have some children, preado-lescents, or adolescents who have attention disorders, or

IT IS VERY DANGEROUS TO CREATE A SENSE OF BOREDOM IN RELATION TO THE GOSPEL

who have too much sugar in them to be able to sit still for a whole meeting. Your entire team should be aware that to expect them to remain seated all the time without moving and without talking to those next to them, is.... not very spiritual. Are you surprised by my statement? I apologize. Well,... no, I don't. Perhaps you expected me to tell you how to make them sit still throughout the meeting. But the truth is, if that is our plan, it is the wrong plan. Movement and surprise are especially useful for restless people and for those who have a hard time focusing.

Considering the changes that are happening in their tracks of develop-ment, and the huge amount of stimuli young people receive through their devices, television, movies, and the ever-present video games, the time has come for us to realize that we cannot continue using the same old strategies and unrealistic expectations that do not respect God's design.

I was having lunch with a group of well-known pastors from a city, and the only youth pastor present heard me talk about this change of expectations. He said to me in a challenging tone that the only important thing was the word, and that it was the only thing we should be paying attention to. I sensed his need for belonging, given the environment, and told him that I completely agreed, but then asked him what he meant when he referred to "the word." He was silent for some time, and then struggled to refrain from saying the phrases that were straining to leave from his mouth. He realized where my question was going. "The word," strictly speaking, is Christ. He is the verb, the logos, the way, the truth and the life. Not even the Bible is these things, much less a simple methodology of communication called "preaching." Christ has to be the most important thing in everything we do, and we must communicate his will and his purposes, which he left us as our mission, and we can and must do it in fresh and surprising ways. Especially when considering the enormous competition we have in trying to captivate and maintain the attention of the new generations in the face of everything the world has to offer.

Any other ideas to come up with surprises? You can have the leaders visit one of their students without previous warning. You can inform their parents of what you are going to do, and wake their children on a Saturday morning to interview them, see their dog, their school notebooks, and whatever might be funny, recording everything on video and then sharing it at the following meeting. You can announce that for some time every Saturday you will surprise someone different. You can work with some parents and adults at the church to prepare a nice dinner to open the meeting. It can be pizza, spaghetti, hamburgers, tacos, or whatever you eat in your city, preferably something simple to prepare. Keep the doors closed for some time before the meeting starts, and place your taller volunteers outside to hold off those who want to enter. (It's funny, but when they can't come in is when they want to come in the most.)

Have the volunteers dress up as cooks or something fun, and they should stay in a good mood while trying to keep the children or teenagers waiting outside. Inside, prepare tables with tablecloths so they can sit down and, after a few minutes (not too long), open the doors and welcome them to the surprise dinner. Serve the food as quickly as possible, and don't be afraid to stop serving after some time. In this way, in addition to surprising them, you will be sending a message to those who come late (they missed the meal), and will avoid further distractions during the rest of the program. The theme for the night? Solid food (1 Corinthians 3).

CREATE SHORT AND CHANGING COMPETITIONS

A bit of competition creates an adrenaline rush. It's impossible to deny that many of us earthlings have a competitive child inside of us. In some cases he or she can be an ugly and destructive monster, and that's why we have to learn to tame them. The fact is that although we cannot give the competitive inner soul free rein, it's also foolish to deny his existence and to refuse to make him useful. God put that child inside of us so we can have fun, so we can learn to establish relationships within a team, and to bring out the best in us. So to provide some healthy competition is useful to energize all types of activities. What good retreat has not used a certain dose of competition? The same can be taken to the rest of the activities in the generational ministry. At some churches it has worked to have a certain number of fixed teams annually, competing to win a top prize at the end of the year. (Of course, the leaders recommend that the prize be really good, to enable the students to maintain their enthusiasm throughout the year.) Another option is to have monthly competitions, or even some that last just one day, or even just a short while, with continuously changing teams, to encourage new friendships in the process. However it may be done, playing is very important for ministries with children, preadolescents, adolescents and youth. The games facilitate interaction; generate camaraderie; provide enthusiasm; and exercise mental, physical, and emotional skills that would not come to light in the classic position of staring at the back of the neck of the one who's sitting in front of them.

The author of Ecclesiastes said that there is a time to laugh and a time to dance (Ecclesiastes 3:1–4), and it is obvious that as Christians we have much to celebrate! We can celebrate by playing games or creating activities that break the ice, and that's where the competitions between teams are very helpful.

Of course, when talking about competition we are not talking about encouraging fights. Some ideas to keep the competition in focus are:

- Change the teams between activities. The longer a team stays together, the more seriously they will take the competition.

- Change between natural teams (for example, men against women), and artificially created teams.

- Use different criteria to assemble the teams (for example: by month of birth, by school, by age, by favorite music, by favorite celebrity, by chance, by surprise under the seat).

- If the score becomes too lopsided toward one side, have the game decided by the last play. That way everybody has the same chance at winning, and the emotion increases because it will come down to one play.

- Let us not become too intense ourselves. It is very common to see leaders who are so passionate about competition that they lose control and ruin what should be a healthy environment.

- Keep in mind the purpose of the activity. Whether it is to integrate, have fun, or illustrate a principle or theme, we must not forget why we are doing it. This will help us maintain the right attitude.

- If you know that a particular sport or game will be difficult to control, avoid it.

- When there are large teams, make sure you have "undercover" volunteers. That is, young people or leaders whom you trust, working so the new generations participate in their teams and keep the right attitude. I say "undercover" because they should not necessarily be on the teams as official leaders, but will simply be participating like everyone else. But you will know that they understand the purpose behind the competition.

USE COMMUNITY RESOURCES

Earlier we talked about "templism." Too many times we limit ourselves when visualizing our ministries outside the church building, and this adds unnecessary constraints to our possibilities.

Hearing me talk about these ideas, on more than one occasion in different countries, pastors approached me to explain that, for example, they were unable to do sports activities because they did not have a gym, and I remember once that a leader who told me this had a nice park only three blocks away from his congregation.

In almost every neighborhood and city there are plenty of resources that generational leaders must learn to take advantage of. It is amazing how many spaces and locations could gladly benefit our programming for the new generations if only we started to look around us a little bit. In some cases you will have to go and sit down with those people responsible for the resources to explain to them our purposes. Often this can even serve to bear witness of Christ. And, above all, it serves to keep the congregation from having that mysterious halo that it sometimes has for nonbelievers.

Jim was a young pastor experiencing his first year at a hyperconservative church, and he asked me how he could have more attractive meetings in a temple that was so old and cold. Of course I asked him, surprised, why he could not change the decorations in his Church building a little to make it warmer. He replied that it would take time, because the people at his church were comfortable like that and that he was finding it very difficult to make the changes that he wanted. Then I asked him why he didn't start taking his youth and adolescent meetings special somewhere else if what he wanted was to avoid the temple.

Some time later I met him again, and he told me that, thinking about what I had said, he had met with the principal of the elementary school that was located at the other corner of his block, and for the first time decided to visit the institution. He was surprised to find that just a few yards away from his own temple there was a beautiful

THE MOST RELEVANT CHURCHES ARE THE ONES THAT ARE WELL CONNECTED TO THE COMMUNITIES IN WHICH THEY ARE LOCATED

assembly hall, with wooden floor and folding chairs, ideal to have activities for adolescents, and that it was available on Saturdays (the most common day for Hispanic youth Church gatherings). Then he told me how it took some courage for him to talk to the principal and ask for the place in exchange for working on some repairs that it needed, and he was able to get it. Jim was happy about his experience, and told me with a huge smile that his young people were happy, that the ministry had multiplied, and that even the most narrow-minded brothers at the church were collaborating, because he had discovered that their problem was not really with the changes, but only with the changes within the temple... because the previous pastor had insisted so much that the place was the holy altar where God's presence lived, so he realized that this was the barrier he had to learn to dodge.

I don't know if it's possible for you to be given a school auditorium in your community, but I do want to encourage you to look beyond the borders of your Church building to see what's available that you can use. While traveling throughout the world I have observed again and again that the most relevant churches are the ones that are well connected to the communities in which they are located.

Think outside the building:

- Is there a municipal office for children or youth in your city? Many municipalities or cities have a government office to work with the new generations. In many cases, even for political reasons, these offices will be willing to help you get land, permits, or discounts for charity work or even evangelistic events.

- Museums: Do you have any museums nearby? Remember what we talked about regarding intellectual development. Although at first it may sound like something boring, it could be very interesting, and allow you to organize a very different type of outing.

- Amusement parks: That amusement park or fair that's nearby can be perfect for a special outing with your discipleship group. Does it have a cost? Try talking to its manager or sales office, and tell him how many children you would bring and what kind of group they are. You might get a discount.

- Adolescents center: Some hospitals or clinics have centers or departments for youth. In these places you can find two things: One is doctors and/or psychologists who can help give a class on sexual education or youth problems. Of course, you should check in advance what they'll be communicating to your group, but there are some neutral subjects that a non-Christian can perfectly address (for example, venereal diseases, how AIDS is spread, bulimia and anorexia, and others). The other thing you may find in these centers is afflicted young people, and they will provide you an excellent opportunity to be of service.

- School classrooms: In addition to the example above, there are many things that can be organized at a school. I know of a church that began offering vocational guidance courses to boys of high school age. Another idea is to offer assistance or support to children and adolescents who have a difficult time with their studies. In many cities, when children are about to fail, their parents pay for private tutors to help them in a specific subject. How about offering that service for free, or at a low cost, using the talents of members of the congregation who can help? Without a doubt, offering something like this will attract the attention of many parents, who will start being grateful to the church.

- Squares, parks, and even cinemas, when there is a movie that lends itself to go see it with the age group we serve.

TAKE ADVANTAGE OF EXTERNAL EVENTS

After hearing me talk about the importance of establishing strategic alliances between pastors, leaders and congregations within the same city, a youth leader with several years of experience approached me to confess that she had never allowed her church's adolescents to go, or had discouraged them from going, to a very famous conference held for them in her city, because she was afraid that they would compare her to other leaders who'd be speaking there. I congratulated her for such a brave confession, since most of us, when we experience these fears or jealousy, would not dare to admit them. But then I asked her why she had never thought about going with them and turning it into an activity within her own ministry. First she looked at me somewhat confused and told me that, since the congress was for young people and she was a married woman, and she was not interested in the speakers they chose, she had never thought about going because she did not think the event was for her. I smiled, looked into her eyes, and told her that of course it was not directed at her as a consumer, but she could go see it with the eyes of a leader and facilitator in order to create an experience for her adolescents without having to plan too much. She could enroll all her teenagers and they could go with a banner of their congregation or a piece of clothing that identified them as a team. They could assign specific workshops or conferences to later report on what was heard and give a lesson in unity to the organizers of the event. After all, if living a group experience with the rest of the body of Christ in the city was good for her teenagers, then it was also good for her, even if the preachers were not her favorites.

> THERE'S NO NEED FOR US TO BE THE ORGANIZERS OF ALL THE ACTIVITIES THAT WE INCLUDE ON OUR CALENDAR

Of course, we cannot go to every big Christian event that happens near us, and we must be careful and selective when choosing which ones to participate in, but there's no need for us to be the organizers of all the activities that we include on our calendar. Supporting the work of other congregations and officially benefiting from the efforts of other Christian organizations is a good measure of stewardship of our time and effort. If someone blesses the new generations you are trying to serve, then that someone is your ally and not your competitor.

> IF SOMEONE BLESSES THE NEW GENERATIONS YOU ARE TRYING TO SERVE, THEN THAT SOMEONE IS YOUR ALLY AND NOT YOUR COMPETITOR

You can even look further and notice that in your city there are cultural, educational, patriotic or even sporting events that you can also include as official activities of your ministry.

USE TECHONOLOGY TO CONNECT AND NOT JUST TO TRANSMIT

Recent events have shown us the urgent need to visualize a stronger and wiser use of technology for communication. It should be obvious already but for too long most churches have only used it to highlight traditional liturgies instead of pivoting toward interaction.

Generational discipleship is a contact sport. So much of what we know as best practices involves a combination of relational work, hosting spaces of community with the new generations, and technology can be an enabler of this reality instead of an alternative to showcase Church building meetings.

All over the globe during the COVID-19 pandemic, for example, children's and youth workers rushed to learn how to use different tech solutions to move weekly gatherings online but many fall prey of trying to transmit a traditional gathering instead of using these tools for personal conversations, and some found that too many students were not engaging with those online approaches.

Many teenagers are weirded out by the conferencing options. They don't like when they can't tell who's looking at them, or who isn't.

On top of this, most online approaches are only workable for families with financial means, leaving out those without computers or smart phones. So the principle about technology is that it should be used as a vehicle of what is already real, a facilitator for what is important and as a means and not an end or a replacement when big group meetings are not possible.

Chapter 8

THE RELATIONAL NUANCE

Only a disciple makes disciples.

A. W. Tozer

I have read dozens of books on discipleship, and traveling through so many corners of the church in practically the entire world, I have found many more approaches to discipleship than I can remember. However, I can summarize the essence of discipleship in a "no" and a "yes."

No: It is not a program.

Yes: It is a relationship.

Discipleship includes activities, but it cannot be limited to a package of activities presented in a precise order, and that is why I do not think it can be considered a "program." What can be observed every time, whenever there is discipleship, is that there is always a relationship. There is always someone who says, out loud or subconsciously, what Paul tells the Corinthians in his first letter to them, at the beginning of chapter 11: "Imitate me, as I imitate Christ." And this can only happen in the context of a relationship.

FROM PROCLAMATION TO EDUCATION

Have you ever asked yourself why some of us spent years at a church and never finished learning some fundamental doctrines of the Christian faith? I did, and I also have asked this question to pastors and leaders all over the world. The most common answer I have heard is that today too often we preach what people want to hear, and not what we should be preaching. But then I ask myself the questions: Does this have anything to do with intentions? Is it true that there are very few pastors or teachers who want to teach us what they know they have to teach?

Perhaps we cannot fault exclusively the pastors or teachers, and it would also be unfair to generalize. Perhaps the fault is in the method.

After my second round of research about neuroscience, I started working on this diagram, which I call "the pentagon of learning."

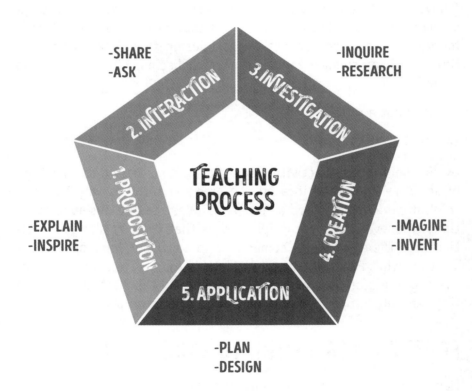

These are the elements that, according to today's pedagogy, should always be present in a creative classroom. That is why I found it important to include this pentagon here, to make it easier for us to see the ideal process to be used with those whom we have the privilege of discipling. This sequence represents the teaching map to which the world's most advanced universities aspire. And, to the surprise of some, we can see Jesus using each of these elements in his discipleship ministry to the new generation.

Don't you think that this pentagon should also be reflected in the pedagogy of the church?

Usually we stay stuck in step 1, naively waiting for people to get to step 5. We proclaim. We announce. We inspire. And, at best, we explain what we may believe and what we should do. But the question was, why don't we get to step 5? And the answer is quite simple. The obvious reason why it is so hard for us to see the application of what we teach is that we skip the various elements necessary to involve the whole brain in learning.

THE BRAIN IS NOT A LARGE ENGINE OF UNDIFFERENTIATED PROCESSES, BUT IT IS ORGANIZED INTO CLEAR AREAS RESPONSIBLE FOR SPECIFIC FUNCTIONS

What science makes clear today is that the nervous system, in its simplest form, works in a kind of action loop. The brain is not a large engine of undifferentiated processes, but it is organized into clear areas responsible for specific functions. That is, different types of stimuli and actions are processed and awaken different neuronal areas that do their job to retain the information and associate it with other information creating knowledge.

The possibility of being able to read the reactions of the left and right hemispheres and even the thalamus and the brain stem through technology has enabled scientists to affirm that listening involves only a few areas of the brain and leaves alone others that are vital for the creation of memories and therefore of values and actions.

WE NEED TO REFORM OUR FORM AND REDISCOVER THAT THE TASK OF THE CHURCH IS NOT CARRIED OUT ONLY WITH PROGRAMS BUT WITH INTENTIONAL RELATIONSHIPS

Look at instances 2, 3 and 4 in the pentagon. Do we create spaces to involve these procedures of alertness and brain involvement with our classic teaching programs? We should, but perhaps we need more than a small update of methodologies, and, in fact, this is the urgency of which we are talking about in this book, and the holistic and complete vision of generational leadership. This is not about having more creative meetings or aesthetically renewing our activities so that more young people come to the services. We need to reform our form and rediscover that the task of the church is not carried out only with programs but with intentional relationships, because many of these elements cannot occur in our traditional activities, but only in the context of a personal face-to-face connection.

Although it is generally assumed that doubting our faith is a bad and even sinful thing, surveys show a different perspective. In studies conducted by Fuller, students who feel the freedom and have the opportunity to express their doubts have a greater predisposition to retain their faith over time, and this illustrates what Lucas is explaining with these ideas.

Unfortunately, too many students who experience doubts remain silent, since our programs, and also our way of building relationships, do not generate the space for that kind of intimacy. Less than half of the students in our research feel that they have the opportunity to share their doubts with adults, or even with other Christian friends.

- Kara

INTENTIONAL MENTORS

My friend Felix Ortiz, whose comments enrich these pages, wrote an excellent book entitled *Every Kid Needs a Mentor*, which I encourage you to read. In it Felix articulates that each young person needs to have adults involved in his or her life who can be examples of what maturity means, and can help them discover the right decisions to make in different circumstances. As we were unlocking in several previous paragraphs, at each stage of our maturation we need to be able to see what's next, and the more examples we can see about how to make decisions the right way, the easier the path will be.

The idea of mentoring comes from the classic Greek work known as *The Odyssey*, written by Homer. In it Ulysses, the main protagonist, has a preadolescent son named Telemachus. Ulysses wants to educate Telemachus to be the future king while he is busy with the Trojan War, so he hires a friend of the family as tutor to Telemachus... and as you can imagine, the name of this man is Mentor.

We all need mentors, and I think that today's children, preadolescents, adolescents, and youth need them more than ever. Perhaps there has never been a time in history, with the exception of periods of war, in which so many children were raised with an absentee parent. Whether it's because of the divorce epidemic,

> **THERE HAS NEVER BEEN A TIME IN HISTORY, WITH THE EXCEPTION OF PERIODS OF WAR, IN WHICH SO MANY CHILDREN WERE RAISED WITH AN ABSENTEE PARENT**

because of the frequency of extramarital children in some communities, or because the consumer society has trained today's men and women to work nonstop in order to buy more things—instead of having as a priority investing time in their children—the fact is that too many children have almost no chance to ask an adult personal questions.

> In John 15:13 Jesus affirmed, "Greater love has no one than this: to lay down one's life for one's friends." There is little chance that one of us will have to lay down his life for another. However, if we think that life is made of time, then the meaning of that passage changes remarkably, and it can be read as follows: "Greater love has no one than this: to give one's time for one's friends." Mentoring is the greatest proof of love we can give a young person or adolescent. It means that we are investing our life in him, so that he can become the person that God had in mind when God created him.
>
> *- Felix*

Let me now remind you that the entire process of transition to adulthood is a succession of stages of searching for a personal identity. We are all born with a genetic, a family, and a cultural heritage, but while we arrive with this package, we all have particular characteristics that will define our individuality. For example, it may be that physically Mary has her father's green eyes and her mother's nose, but her fingerprints are unique. If we add to this that it is God who gives us our spirit, then we can be sure that we are impossible to clone. Each person learns differently, and that has also been one of the main findings of neuroscience.

The sense of identity far exceeds the physical characteristics, and even the IQ, because today we have a more complex understanding that the brain is not just a storage of memory, but that it has a variety of operating principles that determine the functioning of a person. Identity then is like a complex work of art, and that is why "finding oneself" is not an obvious thing to anyone. This is where the close influence of adults modeling maturity is so crucial.

In addition, during the search for identity an experimentation process is carried out that is often very conflictive, especially during adolescence. Many of the great problems that arise at this stage happen when, not having a defined identity, the new generations seek to find themselves by exercising antagonistic roles or by constantly needing to get approval from others.

Sometimes the picture looks like this: One moment she becomes the sexy young woman in social networks, and the next she is the gentle spiritual girl in the church group. One weekend a boy attempts to be a rebellious YouTube DJ, and the following weekend he is the worship leader who looks so spiritual playing his guitar with closed eyes.

As long as the new generations are experiencing this type of dilemma, it is logical that they will feel disgust and dissatisfaction with themselves and with the rest of the world, and this will lead them to use different coping mechanisms, such as:

- Aggression

- Compensation

- Identification

- Rationalization

- Egocentrism

- Evasion

- Escape through sickness

These are just some of the mechanisms that humans use since preadolescence to try to "find ourselves," and they are very difficult to counter with a great sermon.

That's why, once again, it becomes very obvious that the new generations need older people involved in modeling ideal behaviors and aspirations.

Someone who does not know who he is or who he wants to look like can be so unstable that every day he will be on the verge of a mistake with serious consequences, and that is why it is so urgent for them to find mentors who will help them define a positive identity in the light of God's love.

OUTSTANDING EDUCATORS KNOW THAT THEIR STUDENTS NEED FRIENDS WHO ARE IN THE NEXT STEP OF MATURITY

But there's a challenge. Unprepared leaders assume that relationships in the ministry simply happen. They do not work proactively to generate healthy and strong relationships that can be sustained in times of crises typical of the maturation process. These leaders assume that everything can be fixed with strong sermons and improved worship.

On the other hand, outstanding educators know that their students need friends who are in the next step of maturity, and not just inspirational preachers or theologians or "cool" musicians.

That is what relational ministry is about; it's simply an approach to ministry from the intentionality of relationships, always keeping in mind the great goal of accompanying by way of friendship the new generations toward their maturity and God's purposes.

I'll sum it up this way: **The generational vision is intentionally relational.**

I've seen it in action in hundreds of contexts. If we cannot succeed in having the new generations make strong friendships in the church, they will make them outside. And then, in the face of crises or temptations, the chances of losing them or that they'll get hurt along the way will increase exponentially.

IT'S NOT ANOTHER MODEL

The relational nuance is not another ministry model. It is the essence and the nature of effective discipleship. It goes beyond the styles we previously mentioned, because although some of us are less given to relationships than others, if what we want is to train and not just to pass information to our boys and girls, relationships cannot be rejected. Even Paul expressed his relational perspective by saying,

"Because we loved you so much, we were delighted to share with you not only the gospel of God but our lives as well" (1 Thessalonians 2:8).

When someone knows someone else closely, the external tends to disappear, and the true heart of that person starts becoming the main interest when relating to them. This person's brain

THE RELATIONAL NUANCE IS NOT ANOTHER MINISTRY MODEL. IT IS THE ESSENCE AND THE NATURE OF EFFECTIVE DISCIPLESHIP

is exposed to other stimuli that are the results of the example, the opportunity of asking questions and of expressing doubts and fears.

Many Christian pastors, teachers and leaders need to change the way we look at those we have the privilege of influencing. For example:

1. Instead of just seeing them as attendees at our meetings, we should see them as members. When someone has accepted the commitment to follow Christ and has obeyed the church's membership requirements, such as baptism, regardless of age, we must look at him as a member whom we must activate for the work of the kingdom. They cannot be considered simply spectators because of their young age. If God called them to the body, he provided them with gifts (1 Corinthians 7:7), and therefore it is our task to help them find their function within the body. To be able to change our perspective, we as leaders must learn to become humble.

2. Instead of just seeing young people as numbers, we should see them as individuals. I know the pressures that many pastors and leaders face regarding the growth of the church. And I know personally the temptation to only be concerned with having large crowds come to our activities. It is also a fact that the new generations roam in groups, and sometimes it is difficult to distinguish them from each other rather than by the gang or group they belong to. But if we recognize their enormous need for meaningful relationships, and the great opportunity

we have to influence their values during these stages, then it will be easier for us to approach them as individuals. To be able to change our perspective, we must make sure that our motivations are correct.

3. Instead of seeing them as problematic, we should see them as needy. Spending time with those who go from euphoria to indifference, who criticize whatever and whoever they see, and to whom any sound of the electronic device they carry in their pocket can steal away their attention at the most sublime moment in class, is a great challenge. I know many successful communicators who preach to large crowds without any problem, but who would be very nervous if they had to do it before a group of children or preadolescents. Many times at church, young people, children, and especially adolescents and preadolescents only hear complaints about their presence. The administrators complain because they move or break things; deacons complain because the neighbors complain about the noise they make until late at night; the elderly complain because they find shameful the way they dress; some ladies complain because they are easily distracted during the meeting; and on top of all that, other children, adolescents, or young people look at them with suspicion because they do not belong to their small group of friends. To be able to change our perspective we must be more compassionate.

HEALTHY RELATIONSHIPS CLEANSE THE SOUL

Many children and teenagers today live in a world of broken relationships and unprecedented individualism. They learned selfishness from governments, and in society they read pessimism and hopelessness. The social climate of many cities has put people in a bad mood, and it is already known that violence generates more violence. Parents, for their part, are very busy trying to make money, while the children attend schools and colleges where too many teachers do not want to be there, often because their salaries are not enough. The new generations are already going through the natural crises of each stage in their attempts to forge their identity, and this uncertain social climate does not help them at all. The impact of all this means that millions of them suffer severe crises of self-esteem and do not find a place to mend their broken hearts. Sexual pressures from an increasingly shameless industry, and a consumer society where the new generations find themselves dealing with the constant insecurity of short-term relationships, end up staining the fragile souls of those who are discovering themselves.

Think about the impact of divorce. Years of working with teenagers along with my wife allowed me to notice how children who experienced the divorce of their parents tend to have greater difficulty in making decisions about their partners. The environment of betrayal and mutual undermining to which they were exposed by their parents in many cases hurt the children's expectations. In one of the congregations where we had the privilege of pastoring in California, an unmarried couple was on the leadership team, and in both his and her side of the family, all their relatives were divorced. When I realized this, I decided to talk about it directly with them, because I had also noticed that their time of courtship had already been too long. I remember that after talking for a while she told me, "Now I realize that since my preadolescence, I have always thought that if my parents and my siblings were all divorced, nothing can guarantee that I will not fail as well." Thank God, this couple was able to overcome those fears and now they are happily married, but that allowed me to understand the urgency for the church to offer models of courtship and especially positive models of marriage; not perfect, but healthy and credible models.

Who else is going to do it?

The new generations look at the media and there are fewer and fewer good models there. The new generations go to their homes, and too many encounter fragmented families. The school system does not compensate for that need and the government even less. Only the church has the capacity to do it, and once again, that is why we need to review those paradigms inherited from the last century that brought us the idea that the ministry to the new generations is to be handled by leaders who are first-timers and single.

THE PRESENT GENERATION HAS WOUNDS THAT WE MUST HELP HEAL AND WOUNDS THAT WE CAN PREVENT WITH OUR GOOD EXAMPLE

The present generation has wounds that we must help heal and wounds that we can prevent with our good example. Being there, together with them, makes a huge difference in healing their internal blows, redirecting their values altered by some childhood experience, or reconstructing the broken images that they need to grow healthily. If we do not help the new generations handle their emotions that were hurt by their intimate relationships, we will be allowing Satan to paralyze their potential as useful and valuable people. We will be leaving the door open, and with his tricks, Satan will manage to get them to sabotage their own dreams.

Relating closely with people in the process of maturation is not always an easy mission to fulfill, and it requires even more intentionality in the case of ministries that are growing and continuously receiving new members. The consolation is that the techniques and skills of the best relational leaders are based on ideas that are simple, and almost obvious, but incredibly effective.

Devices as simple as:

1. **Remember** the names

2. **Affirm** continuously

3. **Listen** with devotion

4. **Help** to think

5. **Do not pretend** to be perfect.

Let's think about them.

REMEMBER THE NAMES

Their name is one of the most important things each person has. Not knowing someone's name is equivalent to telling them that they are not important enough for us. So if we want students to feel that they are important to us, we must do everything possible to have leaders who do not forget their names. Why would someone whose name we don't remember want to follow our advice? I still find it incredible to see so many churches where people hide behind their "brother/sister" because they never learned the names of others. I don't think there is any family in which true siblings call each other "brother or sister," and definitely this evangelical custom sounds extraterrestrial to outsiders.

Some techniques for remembering names are:

1. Repeat the name quickly as soon as they say it to you.

2. Use the name frequently in the first and subsequent conversations.

3. Use the name before asking a question. ("Charles, what do you think of this?")

4. Match the name with that of someone you already know.

5. Mentally reproduce the image of the person and assign the name consciously after the first time you learned it.

6. Write the name on your phone when you are introduced to someone at the beginning of a meeting, and then mention it during the meeting.

7. Look the person in the eye and then try to remember something special about them.

8. Use group photos to review names.

9. Customize the name with some detail that makes it sound different, taking care that it is not an offensive nickname and

that the person agrees. (This has been one of the techniques I have used the most and I have noticed that having a personal, affectionate name also helps to create closeness.)

10. Make sure the team of teachers and leaders takes this very important task seriously and in team meetings allocate some time to help them do it.

AFFIRM CONTINUOUSLY

We never receive enough encouragement. I don't feel bad to confess that I appreciate when someone notices that I have made a special effort, or listening to loving words when there is no apparent reason. How much more will the new generations appreciate it then?

From childhood to youth, words of appreciation and encouragement achieve much more than we can imagine.

WORDS OF APPRECIATION AND ENCOURAGEMENT ACHIEVE MUCH MORE THAN WE CAN IMAGINE

Today's society spends time enslaving the human being through a very simple but incredibly dangerous premise: that in order to be accepted, recognized and validated, we need some new product that has just been released. The mass media makes the new generations believe that they are not enough and do not have enough until they acquire certain brands or until they have enough followers in their social networks. The supply and demand system works with a well-oiled marketing device that every day tries to convince us that we need something else to feel happy, safe and important. For someone who is in the process of maturing and trying to define his or her identity, it becomes very difficult not to fall prey to the scam, especially considering that the trick not only affects individuals, but it becomes a societal worldview of life that affects the environment of each child and each youth. Classmates are quick to mock, since in a kingdom of insecurity the one who does the most mocking is king. Often parents are also complicit because, with good intentions, they make their children feel bad about themselves because they are not like the children of the happy family in the catalog from the supermarket.

Considering the heavy weight of this reality, someone who shows them appreciation and makes them feel better about themselves is always welcome, and the church can be that place where they receive the encouragement they need to yearn to make the best decisions. Think of values such as integrity, honesty and effort. These attitudes are not received with applause in all corners of our cities. These virtues, along with other positive abilities, should be applauded and affirmed so that they become habits of character in young people.

Some of the aptitudes that we should always recognize and celebrate in the church are:

- Availability

- Honesty

- Obedience

- Sense of humor

- Fidelity

- Punctuality

- Commitment

- Firm convictions

- Compassion

- Good manners and kindness

- Patience

- Giving away the advantage

- General and biblical knowledge

- Humility

- Empathy

- Initiative to approach the new or different

- A sense of justice that defends the unprotected

And there are many more.

Society already celebrates other abilities that we can also celebrate, such as beauty, popularity, athletic or academic performance, but if we do not celebrate those other qualities, we reduce our chances of raising countercultural generations that will influence the world instead of being influenced by it.

LISTEN WITH DEVOTION

In the collective unconscious of the Christian leadership, we have established that our task has more to do with speaking than with listening, and this weakness has delayed the progress of many and has kept too many ministries below their potential.

JUST BY LISTENING A LITTLE MORE, WE CAN GREATLY IMPROVE OUR LEADERSHIP

Some of us are so prone to talk that we find it difficult to listen. We should ask ourselves why God gave us two ears and only one mouth. In the Bible we find James saying, "My dear brothers and sisters, take note of this: Everyone should be quick to listen, slow to speak and slow to become angry" (James 1:19).

Some of us, even in discipleship situations in which we can give advice, miss the opportunity to do so by not listening while the other person speaks, and I wonder: if we cannot listen to someone in need, whom we see, how are we going to listen to God, whom we do not see?

You are absolutely right, Lucas. We must listen with devotion. Youth and adolescents do not need more sermons; they need to be heard. They need someone to transmit courage, dignity, and importance to them, doing something as simple as listening to them in a focused, dedicated way, without judgments or convictions. My wife, Sara, has a phrase that I love: "Listening is a form of hospitality." Hospitality for the soul, something that new generations are so much in need of. Sara and I have proven with amazing frequency that many people just need to be heard, and in that process of feeling heard and welcomed, they themselves rearrange their inner world. Good listening accompanied by potent questions is a very powerful tool to utilize as we accompany our children spiritually.

- Felix

Children, youth and especially adolescents are highly in need of someone to listen to them, and the good news is that, just by listening a little more, we can greatly improve our leadership.

Listening with devotion is an extremely powerful tool and we must note that active listening is not only limited to listening to words, but it is also necessary to be attentive to body language. People are always communicating, even without needing to verbalize what they think or feel, and that's why asking open-ended questions, or highlighting emotions with phrases of empathy like "That must have been terrible," always helps the other person to communicate more clearly.

Some clues to activate our ears in the ministry are:

- Avoid the messianic complex. The role of leaders is not to solve everyone's problems. We are not anyone's messiah and in many situations the best help is just to listen. In many counseling situations there is simply no solution, and in others, it is much better for the preadolescent or youth to find their own solutions.

- Engage in the conversation. Spiritual growth is not mathematics. It demands time, intimacy and trust and not all intimate counseling times end in one session. We must be willing to be there for the long term and not try to fix mistaken feelings and actions in a few minutes of counseling.

- Repeat what you heard. Saying: "I understand that you are saying that..." helps those being counseled to know that you are listening, and enables them to correct themselves if they communicated something in a confusing way.

- Wait for the turn to speak and look people in the face.

- Pay attention to nonverbal language. Positions and gestures sometimes speak clearer than words.

- Keep listening. Let's be honest, it is normal to lose the thread sometimes. Recover by asking a question, and listen again.

HELP TO THINK

One of the values of the precious ministry of which I am a member says that "the questions are as important as the answers" and this is a powerful truth, because our mission is not reduced to telling the new generations what they should think, do, or believe.

THE BEST TEACHERS ARE THE ONES WHO GET THEIR STUDENTS TO REACH THE CORRECT CONCLUSION WITHOUT EVER TELLING THEM WHAT IT IS

The task of the church, and even the family, is to guide students to those truths that we know they must internalize, but we cannot do it for them. They must discover the truths themselves. The best teachers are the ones who enable their students to reach the correct conclusion without ever telling them what it is. Think about that for a while.

Helping to think is not only done with questions, but also with statements that say something to the students' unconscious. Other times it is done by reorienting the emotions of those valuable people under our influence, for example, by raising them up or consoling them after a failure.

These phrases and questions are very useful:

- What do you think God is teaching you with this?
- You can do very well!
- Do not give up!
- What a good idea!
- Tell me more about that.
- Tell me in your own words what you heard me say.
- What do your parents think?
- What are the potential consequences of this?
- What do you like about him/her?
- We are sure that you will make a good decision.
- It's good to talk to you!
- I like having you in the church!

DO NOT PRETEND TO BE PERFECT

The new generations get very discouraged when they see adults who say one thing and do another, and especially for children it is very conflicting to encounter this reality. Their worlds crumble, especially when they somehow believed that we were superheroes who would never do anything wrong. How do we avoid this? By being honest and intentional in teaching them early that we are not perfect and that we are on the same path as they are, even if we are further along.

LET US NOT BE AFRAID TO ADMIT TO THE NEW GENERATIONS THAT WE ARE ALSO CONTINUING TO GROW, AND LEARNING TO MATURE

Some time ago I saw a video of a very famous preacher telling us how the Holy Spirit came to him one day and instantly at that moment all his sins died. Hmmm... What was this preacher saying? His tone sounded very emotional, and as he told it, images of his crusades filled with people appeared, hands raised and crying behind him. (The images had also appeared at the beginning of the video, and when they introduced him.) I wouldn't want to doubt what he was saying, but... think about those words. Can it be true that all his sins died in an instant? Which ones? And, above all, what does that mean for those who hear him? Quite simply, for someone immature, that will mean that this person does not sin, and I do. It means that he no longer struggles with temptations nor has weaknesses, and I do. And with good will I can look for something of this preacher to stick to me for a while, but sooner or later I will reach one of two convictions: either he is lying, or I am a failure.

Perhaps that preacher simply confused his words on that occasion, but leaders must be careful of communicating something that is not real.

It is very healthy to make it clear to the new generations that we have the same need for God and are in the same search for Christ as they are. Thinking about us, hypocrisy is never a good idea; and thinking about them, our honesty will hurt them less when they sooner or later realize that we have not reached perfection either.

In addition, today we live in a different time where not even the heroes of the movies are perfect, as they used to be portrayed, and in the midst of this new social climate a generation of leaders is rising who are more honest than the previous ones. In fact, I remember when almost twenty years ago I started a tour called "Generation Leaders" that took me through 100 cities and more than 20 countries and had a whole session talking about authenticity, I felt as if what I was saying was an extraterrestrial revelation. But today that is no longer the case and I hear the word "authenticity" in pulpits where previously it would have been highly unlikely.

Let us not be afraid to admit to the new generations that we are also continuing to grow, and learning to mature. We are on the same path of discipleship as they are, presumably at a later stage, but we are still all children returning to our Father.

We are disciples who need to be discipled while we disciple others, until we all reach unity in the faith and in the knowledge of the Son of God and become mature, attaining to the whole measure of the fullness of Christ (Ephesians 4:13).

Chapter 9

CULTURAL INTELLIGENCE

The church cannot arrive seven years later.

Charles Spurgeon

Many years ago I had the opportunity to interpret for John Stott, one of the most respected English theologians of the last century, and still today I remember a phrase he said at that conference in Buenos Aires. "Every Christian needs two conversions: one, from the world to Christ; and another, back to the world, but with Christ."

John hit the target. When we deliver every inch of our being to the lordship of Christ, we are embracing his mission of leaving all for the love of others. This is what Paul emphasizes in chapter 2 of his letter to the Philippians. Christ left his culture to immerse himself in ours. He spoke our language, walked our streets, and had to wear our clothes. He limited himself, sleeping in a bed and eating our food, and he even rejoiced and cried with our joys and sorrows.

A key that I have seen work in organizations and even in healthy families is that effective ministries and parents who have the best dialogue with their children make continuous contact with the culture they intend to influence. That is, they learn to "incarnate" using "cultural intelligence." These parents, or these ministries, have leaders with a cunning idea of the things the new generations consume, and the things that interest them. They use contextual codes without altering the eternal message, because they know how to differentiate between what is essential to the evangelical message and what is a matter of forms, traditions, tastes and culture.

Translating eternal messages into modern times with an under-standing of past times can be challenging, and that is why an intel-ligent cultural "incarnation" is so necessary.

THE HISTORY OF A CONTEXT

Every social context has a history. The anthropologist Charles Kraft, of Fuller Seminary, used to emphasize that culture "consists of all the things we learn in the world, after being born, that allow us to func-tion as expected as biological beings in relation to our environment." Time and space set decisive differences when defining a generation, and describing that "environment" brings a lot of light when estab-lishing the best way to influence it.

In many corners of Christianity, we are used to becoming defensive when anything new shows up in the environment. If we do not know what it is, we stand up against it just in case. But there are appre-ciations regarding culture we should learn, without getting scared. I'm not saying that it's of utmost importance for us to get involved in a philosophical discussion about each new aspect, but if these patterns modify the way in which the new generations understand the world, then it is a good idea to pay attention and understand, at least in an introductory way, some of these trends.

Many scholars of the processes of evolution of culture agree that the critique of modernity started by romanticism in the nineteenth century and had its peak with the emergence of a highly corrosive philosopher named Friedrich Nietzsche. Nietzsche criticized morality, defining it as "unnatural" for coming from the mystical idea, according to him, of the existence of a moral God. That is why his best known and remembered statement to this day is, "God is dead."

The anthropocentrism of the Renaissance, the rationalism of Descartes, the power of the people, and the new rise of science, tried to make Nietzsche's claim a confirmed hypothesis, and, in fact, the nineteenth century saw so many structural changes in the conformation of the national states, that an obvious positivism seized the international scene. By that time, one could already sense a general discrediting of the official church, and even of many reform movements. Modernity then erected new ideals, and ideologies arose behind those ideals about how to achieve them, which have remained until today. Some of the ideas going around in that "environment" were:

- Technological and scientific progress would solve humanity's problems.

- The demise of monarchies, the liberal order, or the power of the people would fix the political and social problems.

- Religion would no longer be necessary.

However, in the twentieth century, the assumptions of modernity began to be questioned. Despite the existence of previously unthinkable advances in communication, humans continued to experience isolation and loneliness. After the great wars, the noble ideals of peace attainable through progress were also gone, and with them the interest in participating in projects or "utopias" with the purpose of legitimizing, uniting and bringing into action social movements. The new generations would soon stop believing in the possibility of a project of true change or social revolution, and so we came to what was later known as postmodernity, a time when consumerist individualism, instant satisfaction, and private endeavors fragmented society into many personal interests that fluctuate between supply and demand.

But the story didn't end there either. What always happens with all human cultural stages happened. Postmodernity also began to change. In practical terms, the "new social century" began with the collision of two airplanes into two towers in New York. Suddenly, the West became much more aware of the huge and growing Muslim world. Some years later, millions of refugees arrived in Europe, drastically changing the demographics of many cities. Meanwhile, in some capitals of Latin America, a marked populism was installed, encouraged by the social frustration created by a gap between the haves and the have-nots that brought back the verve of revolution and in

North America and some European countries, a counterpart of this populism was manifested in a movement toward the ultra right.

In the midst of this picture, a new search for the spiritual also emerged, but now outside the traditional religions and with a strong root in alternative stories and even some very local ones from each region. And we cannot forget the new standards of equality, which now include gender and sexuality.

THE MOST SIGNIFICANT CHANGES

Planet Earth's new selfie was found, in the foreground, with the paradox of a globalized world, yet one fragmented into thousands of microcultures that coexist interconnected. Latinos eat sushi, and Thai eat chimichangas. In Sweden the Peruvian restaurants are in, and in Montevideo it's the Armenian. But at the same time, we cannot dismiss the fact that in each city there are thousands of tribes with completely different interests and tastes and even transversal interests shared by someone age 8 or 18 or 28 or 38. That's why in general I can't find it useful to try to make a characterization of complete generations using terms such as Gen X, Millennials, Gen Z or Alpha, since they fluctuate continuously. However, there are some tendencies in thought that influence the behavior of different groups, and that affect the entire focus of generational leadership, so we should stop to analyze them.

FROM ABSOLUTE TO RELATIVE

Behaviors that were previously inadmissible have become yet another option. A university student may ask you, "Who defines what is right and what is wrong within the limits of legality?" You will start to hear more often that there is no longer a pure political left or right, and in pop art there is an insistence that all religions are equally valid. "Beliefs are not absolute, but relative to the circumstances and to each person's convenience," an adolescent may say, without even suspecting that people didn't always think that way. Using the internet you can view the most recent scientific discovery, or the worst violent pornography. Some speak of tolerance, and say that it results in a more just society. Others are up in arms, asking to what extent one cannot be able to exercise any value judgment on the private conduct of others. Does everything have to be relative? Or should everything be absolute? Or... is it possible that the problem lies in including the word "everything" in the questions?

FROM PRODUCTIVITY TO PLEASURE:

To "relax" was considered a bad word just a few generations ago, but today it is an aspiration. In an era where everything has to be right now, there is little room to think about producing for the future. They've been trying to tame the last generations, so that they think only of the now and the search for pleasure. On the opposite pole, our grandparents and their ancestors had a fascination with work and utility. Especially for men, their work related to their identity. Now, the "I must do" has been replaced by the "I want to feel." Never before in history have there been so many forms of physical entertainment, so many different tastes, so many virtual experiences, so many products, so many clothes. The pleasure industry grew bigger, and it altered our scale of values. Life will become more and more comfortable, but this change will shape our way of thinking and also our yearnings. Those European immigrants who came to America to sweat working the land are already long gone. Immediate pleasure and effortless results seem to be the perfect equation for today. But it was not always like this.

As parents, it is natural that the last thing we want is for our children to experience pain. But, as Paul writes in Romans 5:3-4, "We know that suffering produces perseverance; perseverance, character; and character, hope." Of course I would prefer it not to be this way, but pain is one of God's main avenues for the growth and formation of identity.

We can help our sons and daughters by being attentive to particular events that incite crises that facilitate their growth, such as a loss in the family, an argument with a close friend, or a challenge in their studies. Of course, not all difficulties will be big problems from the perspective of adults, and many of the difficulties will be new questions about their faith, or new patterns of disobedience in everyday details, or the normal stress brought about by an important event in their calendars. Each of these small difficulties presents a valuable opportunity to help them grow and learn to trust in the God who made them.

-Kara

FROM INTIMACY TO TECHNOLOGY

Surely it will have happened to you more than once that you are in a conversation with someone who is paying attention to you, until their cell phone rings and that person simply takes a mental plane to another place. Today, when talking about friends, we differentiate between web friends and personal friends. The problem is that, with this barter, the latter seem to become more and more scarce, and contacts through social networks become ubiquitous. The bad thing perhaps may not be to have friends on the web. The bad thing is to replace relationships of intimacy, artificially supplanting them with distant relationships with people who can make us feel all kinds of different sensations by creating false or at least incomplete realities. This is also not new, nor does it have to do exclusively with social networks, nor is it really the fault of the new generations. Children learn from their parents, and when parents cannot sit down to eat without a TV on, and we cannot control the urge to answer the phone no matter who we are with or what we are talking about, the children see in us that technology is a priority. It is the bigger fish that is eating the smaller ones.

FROM REBELLION TO INDIFFERENCE

The latter part of the last century was a time of school protests, rock music, shrill fashions, and teenage rebellion. The first environmental movements emerged, and the standard was to oppose. In fact, it didn't matter much what to rebel against, but it had to be done. Rebelling was a sign of cultural status.

Since forever, the new generations were considered the greatest force of social change, and for decades they were in charge of shouting it to the four winds. But despite the protests, the colors and the changing rhythms,

A GENERATION THAT LIVES TAKING SELFIES AND POSTING PERSONAL VIDEOS CONTINUOUSLY GETS USED TO FOCUSING ON THEIR OWN STORY INSTEAD OF TRYING TO CHANGE THE PICTURE OF THEIR SOCIAL CONTEXT

society kept moving in the direction of corruption and consumerist materialism, and the result was that the new generations installed in their collective unconscious a philosophy of "who cares?" Today, when I talk to adolescents and ask them what they think of society and politics, there are too many who prefer not to give their opinion. But I have observed that if I insist on the question, soon there is a reply such as: "They are all corrupt" or "It is not worth it to get involved" or "Politicians say what people want to hear, but they only care about themselves." Of course, there are "cultural islands" here and there, where something mobilizes new generations to act or to manifest themselves publicly, but the momentum is usually short-term and not a vocation, as it was in previous decades. A generation that lives taking selfies and posting personal videos continuously gets used to focusing on their own story instead of trying to change the picture of their social context.

FROM FAMILY TO MULTIFAMILY

Different statistics indicate that one third of the world's children go to bed without a father in the other room. In light of what we have already discussed, you can imagine the negative impact that this makes. When I lived with my family in the city of Miami, I observed that among ten friends of my children, only one had his natural father and mother at home. Regardless of what may have caused each family breakup, God wants us to share his love and his power with this generation, taking into account the situation in which they find themselves. A lot of material for Bible studies, and many sermons, forget to take into account how many children and youth who are in the church live this reality, and without wanting to, we can be impractical, or add guilt on the backs of those who inherited this problem. The children of these families have siblings shared with other fathers and mothers, and are often raised by stepfathers and stepmothers who have not assimilated that, by marrying their new partners with children, these children are evaluating them as parents and, consciously or unconsciously, are internalizing many of their values.

FROM LEGACY TO FAME

There have always been famous people, but fame has not always been an objective, or even an obsession, for so many people. You have probably seen on TV or on the web that social experiment in which someone—any person—walks through a busy street surrounded by people—who are actually hired extras—who take pictures and ask for autographs. Invariably, a few minutes later there are already other people—regular people, who do not know that it is an experiment—who begin to approach to ask for autographs and take pictures with this someone although, obviously, they have no idea who he is (because he really is nobody famous). Isn't this something to think about?

What effect does this "sensationalism" and this fascination with "fame" have on our vision of life and our scale of values? History records that until a few decades ago most people longed to leave a legacy and enjoy a meaningful life, but fame did not appear on the agenda of the bulk of the population. That has changed, and today we give so much value to fame, that there are even cases of people who are famous only for being famous, as you can see with some "stars" of reality shows who as far as we know don't have any talents other than having been on TV and being... famous! This tendency has also gotten in through the windows of the churches, and in some circles spirituality has been measured by the number of followers in social networks. I have been saddened to hear Christian leaders say, as if it's no big deal, that they choose their guests for different events based on "who brings more people," without suspecting that this reveals a superficial criterion that has nothing to do with blessing people or achieving an objective beyond sharing the fame of the famous.

FROM EDUCATION TO SPECIALIZATION

The motto of my high school was "to know is power." It was not clear what it was that we needed to know. We just had to know, and with that idea the study programs were put together. "Education" meant to acquire general knowledge of all types and subjects. And as we progressed in our studies we were acquiring a little of many things, without knowing much of anything. Today the labor market requires specific things, and education has been changing. Will this have any impact on the church? Surely it does for families. It is significant to note that in countries where most of the technological and even theoretical-scientific advances are generated, children may have little general knowledge, but from a young age they become specialists in something. I believe that this should also affect ministerial education, and that is why at e625 we created an online institute from the perspective of generational leadership (www.InstitutoE625.com)

but like all the other cultural changes this has its own dangers. Many kids become so deeply entrenched inside their chosen discipline at an early age that they can lack critical thinking skills to better evaluate reality outside of that specialization.

For many of them, the foundations of their minds are laid early within their education by the initial introductory courses that are mandatory; from which follows another three or four years of thorough training within that discipline. In addition, the courses that become available past the initial years demand even more of the person, and so the time that can be allocated to extracurricular education becomes even more scarce. So, to perform well in their discipline, they need to spend all their available time studying their disciplines texts; therefore, in a sense becoming culturally programmed within one area of life and detached from a more fluent and emphatic worldview.

FROM RELIGION TO SPIRITUALITY

You turn on the TV today and even the children's programs are full of mysticism. There are demigods, demons, angels, and spirits, acting as heroes or villains of countless children's and teenagers' series. You will also notice it in video games. Many fashion artists say they consider themselves "spiritual," and even talk about "God" in award shows or in their songs, but their moral life makes it clear that their "god" doesn't have much connection with their personal morality.

I recently asked a group of teenagers who did not attend church about this, and they replied that they thought it was not right, but that they understood it because, according to them, "nobody could judge what God wants." Contradictory, right? In addition, many of them did not believe in churches, or pastors, or priests, but said they did have contact with God, and that they went to church when they wanted to ask for something or to make God a promise, sometimes in exchange for something.

The fact is that to imply that someone is spiritual is well accepted in most media. However, to say that someone has a lot of religion sounds bad even in the corners of a church. And this was not always the case either.

FROM CONVICTIONS TO SENSATIONS

A few decades ago the church admired theologians. Then the stars were the evangelists, and today in many circles the celebrities are the artists or the preachers who behave like them. What is behind this change? No doubt there is a lot of influence from the secular world, and the effect of fame, that we already mentioned. But here the barter between the absolute and the relative also comes into play since, if truths are personal, what defines them does not come from outside but from within, from our own sensory perception. So, is there something wrong with feelings? Of course not; they are not wrong in and of themselves. But feelings depend on changing stimuli, and therefore to develop a firm will you cannot depend on such stimuli, but on firm and obviously healthy stimuli, such as convictions. Kids with stronger convictions better regulate their emotions and make more reliable decisions. This is true above all when those convictions are anchored in the word of God.

> KIDS WITH STRONGER CONVICTIONS BETTER REGULATE THEIR EMOTIONS AND MAKE MORE RELIABLE DECISIONS

THE DANGER OF MONOCULTURALISM

The belief that our culture and our social environment are the only reference and the only framework of interpretation of reality is a severe disadvantage. It puts us on the defensive and moves us away from dialogue.

The history of missions is full of testimonies from women and men of God who discovered the beauty of seeing Jesus act in a culture that's different from their own. These people realized that many of the things they thought were important were not as important from the point of view of the needs of the others, and they understood the multiculturalism of a gospel that responds to all human needs.

ALL OF US NEED CULTURAL INTELLIGENCE TO FULFILL THE MISSION THAT GOD PLACED IN OUR HANDS

From a specific personal standpoint, I have much to thank God for having studied in two different countries, having served in congregations of different sizes and denominations, and for the opportunities I continue to have to travel. Traveling has allowed me to see with international eyes and listen with regional ears. This, in turn, has allowed me to read thought tendencies in the people I lead, which enables me to make a situational application of the different leadership styles in order to lead better. It also brings me to mercy, because I understand why a certain word or action offends in one context, while in a different context the same word or action goes completely unnoticed. There is always a contextual story behind it, and knowing how to read that frame of reference allows me to better decide how I should speak and conduct myself in one context or another.

WITHOUT NEGLECTING THE MICRO, WE MUST HAVE A MACRO VIEW

What we need to make clear in this chapter is that all of us need cultural intelligence to fulfill the mission that God placed in our hands, particularly in regard to the new generations. The mission to the new generations does not always require geographical leaps, but it does demand many intergenerational and cultural leaps. Without neglecting the micro, we must have a macro view, and this cannot be reduced to making our meetings aesthetically more attractive to new generations. We must understand the interpretive framework of our audience, and we must bear in mind the invitation that Jesus made to his disciples to be the salt of the earth and the light that casts out the darkness (Matthew 5:13–15).

The author of the letter to the Hebrews connects the incarnation of Christ to a long history of events in which God took the initiative to contextualize with the people he loves, in culturally intelligent ways. The letter begins by saying: "In the past God spoke to our ancestors through the prophets at many times and in various ways, but in these last days he has spoken to us by his Son" (Hebrews 1:1–2). In other words, the author is stressing that God's way has respected different times to communicate differently, and that in Jesus he has found his most relevant way of communicating. As the Gospel of John says, Jesus is the verb of God. His incarnation is the ultimate expression of contextualization! The commitment to express love so that the other can understand that love is one of the main hallmarks of Christianity, and differentiates our approach to faith from any other approach of diverse religions that were raised by man.

CHRISTIANITY IS MULTICULTURAL BECAUSE JESUS SPEAKS THE LANGUAGE OF ALL CULTURES

Christianity is multicultural because Jesus speaks the language of all cultures, and because he is the word that everyone can understand, even children.

Without ever ceasing from looking at Jesus, we have to look at the world of the new generations through the eyes of contextualization. We must approach them with empathy and a sweet mixture of compassion and understanding, respecting their tastes and harmonies, and avoiding the sin of monoculturalism, which imposes and overwhelms with traditions that have nothing to do with the sacred.

GOD'S LANGUAGE

God's language is always Jesus.

The great Danish philosopher and theologian Søren Kierkegaard said that to love another person is to help them to love God, and I cannot agree more with that simple and profound idea.

TO ACT WITH CULTURAL INTELLIGENCE IS AN INVITATION TO RELIVE THE EVANGELISM OF THE CHURCH OF THE FIRST CENTURY

It is true that contemporary culture has invited millions to live surrendered to the moment, and indifferent to everything that requires a lifestyle that involves the risk of feeling pain. But not everything is negative. The new generations have the nagging suspicion that a genuine spiritual experience is possible, and we should take hold of that suspicion with devotion.

Evangelization in the coming years will depend much more on the testimony of love than on having a good list of doctrines sweetened with evangelistic formulas and packaged in a cool liturgy.

The new generations want to see that we live what we preach, in a frame of reference that they can interpret. The fact that they are unwilling to settle for an argumentative explanation, and instead want to feel something special, is an advantage and not merely a challenge, because the gospel is the power of God that strikes the mind and captivates the heart.

> *Postmodernity scholars talk about a very important concept: credibility structures. According to them, in the postmodern world (characterized by a plurality of options and lifestyles) only those who have a credibility structure that supports them have the ability to survive, that is, within a community that lives and embodies the principles and values that a particular lifestyle defends and proclaims. In other words, unless the church is a credible structure for the gospel, there is little or no hope that the new generations will embrace it.*
>
> *- Felix*

To act with cultural intelligence is an invitation to relive the evangelism of the church of the first century, a Christian experience of relationships and the power of mercy, as we read in Acts

2:44–47. The times in which we live invite Christian chuches to be less sermon-centric and more open and relational, to involve the new generations in our Christian homes. The challenge that lies ahead is to get children, preadolescents, adolescents and young adults to fall in love with the possibility of seeing, liking and feeling a gospel that can be translated into everyday life, a gospel that they can talk about with their school friends, and that answers the needs of all the families in a community.

> I am not sure if we are sufficiently aware of how much of our theology and culture contributes to the church's interactions with our secular context. Teenagers and emerging adults can feel our theology, even if we never use that term.
>
> Recruit your leadership team and some high school and college youth to discuss three critical questions:
>
> What do our actions and communications (web, videos, messages, advertisements, schedules) explicitly or implicitly reveal to the outside world about our identity?
>
> What exactly do we believe about how we should interact with the culture and the world around us?
>
> If by comparing what we believe and what we communicate we notice some inconsistencies, what can we do to become better neighbors in the place where God put us?
>
> *-Kara*

If you take the time to reread the tendencies of change that we've been analyzing in our observation of reality, you can see that there are several characteristics of our time that are simply neutral in moral terms, and that represent an opportunity for improvements in the church. Think, for example, of the change from education to specialization, and the practical connotations that it has for the development of individuals and for the maximization of the possibilities of your congregation. Think about technology, and imagine how it

THE LIGHT OF THE GOSPEL IN US CANNOT REMAIN HIDDEN BEHIND TRADITIONS THAT ARE NOT CONSISTENT WITH THE CULTURAL CONTEXT

can become a means to facilitate our teaching task, while allowing us to connect with the frame of reference of the new generations and generate spaces for them to become an active part of the church.

The story of the manger and the cross is the most decisive narrative in human history. It is the story of God becoming a man to make himself relevant to a humanity that needs him.

When looking at the parables, it is clear that Jesus used all kinds of codes to highlight his truth. And Paul even used the altar to a pagan god to bring the attention of a community to Christ (Acts 17:22–24). Now it's our turn to practice that cultural intelligence in order to convey the message to the new generations.

Just as a city on top of a hill cannot be hidden, the light of the gospel in us cannot remain hidden behind traditions that are not consistent with the cultural context in which God chose to make us shine.

Chapter 10

THE BEAUTY OF CHANGE

Faith makes all things possible.... Love makes all things easy.
Dwight L. Moody

The keys to action proposed in this book are essential to direct the ministries of our local churches toward the results that we can and must achieve. In summary, we can diligently work together to standardize the following four best practices for our ministries:

- Relevant pastoral
- Integrated strategy
- Active families
- Intentional discipleship

The enemies we face are enormous. Busy parents, archaic methods, visions rooted in ancient traditions, insufficient budgets, and the invasion of cultural values foreign to the gospel on all fronts of attack. But we can't settle with excuses. It is possible, and it is urgent, to implement these ministerial views in our faith communities.

> *Do not fear change! The entire creation teaches that living beings are constantly changing and, let us not forget, the church is described in the Bible as a living being, a family, a body. Even when it is described as a building, it is one made of living stones!*

Biology teaches us that living things change when faced with two great challenges: an opportunity to grow or a threat to their survival. In addition, to be able to change they use a mechanism called "self-reference." That is, they are very clear about their DNA, and therefore they can change completely and absolutely their external form while keeping their internal identity intact. The exterior may be difficult to identify, but their DNA remains exactly the same. It remains unaltered.

This is of urgent application for the church today. We must be very clear about our DNA, so that we can face change without any fear of losing our identity. If identity is defined by our programs, activities, materials, rules, etc., then we may find it impossible to change. However, if our identity is determined by our mission—to help integrate Jesus in people's lives, and build the kingdom of God—then we can change very easily, because we only have to answer one question: "What is the most effective and efficient way to carry out our mission in this context in which the Lord has placed us?"

- Felix

CHANGES IN METHODS AND STRATEGIES ARE FIRST CREATED IN THE INTELLECT, THE HEART AND THE IMAGINATION OF THE LEADERS

In the first appendix at the end of the book you will find an implementation guide that considers the perspective of pastors, of youth leaders and of child care providers. The guide includes practical steps to lead a transition in missional architecture in our congregations, but before doing that, the most important thing we can do is to pause and look at the change in our vision, since changes in methods and strategies are first created in the intellect, the heart and the imagination of the leaders.

THE VISION OF A NEW REALITY

Let's go back to the basic diagram of the dynamics of generational leadership.

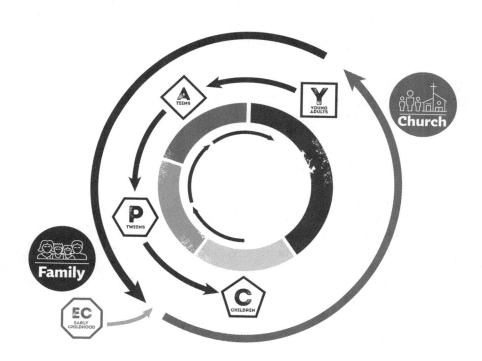

RELEVANT PASTORAL

Each phase of development needs a relevant pastoral approach. We can develop programs and relational vehicles by being sensitive to God's design of each stage of life, and the more scientific and experimental information we can internalize regarding the public we serve, the better we can do it. Beloved pastor, leader, mom, dad, or educator, walk through your church building and think about the programs, looking at them with the eyes of the new generations.

What do they see in those classrooms, in those corridors, and in the main sanctuary? Imagine what type of environment and significance they yearn for, and think about what you can do to get them involved, taking into account the stage they are in.

In the diagram as in real life, the early childhood is the entry door but is not moving in the cycle because, in terms of programs, the church as an institution is unable to do much work directly with the youngest ones, although what it can do is encourage parents to devote to their fragile children the urgent attention they need, starting to create spaces for them to feel safe in a Christian environment as soon as they reach the preschool stage.

INTEGRATED STRATEGY

We must stop planning our efforts in isolation. We need good transitions between stages and that is why we cannot have a divorce between the children's ministry and the youth ministry, or not think about preadolescents and their transition to adolescence.

We must include them in the service teams to give them significance and generate belonging, and at the same time, allow minors to have a concrete model worthy of imitating of the next stage of maturity that they will go through.

Islam does this very well, especially with confrontation groups that are considered terrorists in the West, such as the Islamic State and other subgroups. Have you ever wondered how these groups are able to threaten the main military powers of NATO and resist continuous strife in spite of an abismal difference in weaponry? Those young people we see in the news are willing to die for their cause. The strength of these groups is not in weapons but in how they train and disciple their new generations. In other words, while in the West we hold meetings, they use a gradual orientation model very similar to what we are calling generational leadership where a twelve-year-old child trains a six-year-old while an eighteen-year-old commands a twelve-year-old.

We need to stop treating each stage the same and we need to start integrating them wisely. What was done in the last century was done in the last century. The time has come to

PARENTS ARE THE MAIN INFLUENCE IN THE LIVES OF THEIR CHILDREN, BUT THEY ARE NOT THE ONLY ONE THEY NEED

plan better transitions between childhood, preadolescence, adolescence and the college stage, and that is why it is essential that those who work with these age groups work interconnected and with common goals, supervised by pastors involved in the vision of their congregation when it comes to working with the new generations.

ACTIVE FAMILIES

The family can never be on the periphery of our ministries; it should be at the center of our attention. It is impossible to achieve the powerful results that we must achieve without taking into account the relationship between the new generations and their parents. Parents must gain prominence in our ministerial vision, and it is possible that parents and educators working together will make the best team by accompanying the new generations in their spiritual formation.

Parents are the main influence in the lives of their children, but they are not the only one they need, and that is why the church will be able to play a leading role in the socialization of the new generations toward mature adulthood. Christian educators of all levels must embrace and prioritize the attention that the new generations require. A church that does not do this will age without generational change and will endanger its future and that of the new generations that it had the opportunity to influence.

INTENTIONAL DISCIPLESHIP

Let's repeat it for the umpteenth time: The goal of the church is not to have good meetings and fill up the church building with people with good doctrines. Our mission is to make disciples, and Jesus' disciples are good citizens, good employees, good employers, good entrepreneurs who generate social improvements, and good parents.

> Many of the students interviewed for different surveys by Fuller Youth Institute admitted that they had put their faith "on hold" during their university years so they could have fun and enjoy themselves during this stage, thinking that perhaps when they reached adulthood they would recover their faith. We can translate this to mean that their Christian environment taught them that their faith was not compatible with a transcendent life, a fun life or an abundant life, let alone a Christianity that has positive social consequences. This must be changed, because a Christianity that does not work, "will not work," and that is why the task of the church and the paradigm changes that Lucas is proposing are so crucial.
>
> *-Kara*

GOD BELIEVES IN THE DISCIPLESHIP OF NEW GENERATIONS MORE THAN WE DO

A church that knows how to impact the new generations with cunning and fidelity not only will have a vibrant congregation, but also will affect its surroundings. This is the church our communities need! Schools and universities, neighborhoods and governments, everyone needs these types of churches! Congregations that rescue, nourish and alter the course of life of the new generations, enabling more and more children, preadolescents, adolescents and youth to reach mature adulthood in Christ are vital.

God believes in the discipleship of new generations more than we do. We can rest in his grace, fight his battles with his strength, and throw ourselves confidently into the bold vision of generational leadership.

HEAVEN IS PAYING ATTENTION

Nothing important can be rushed, and inevitably we will go through difficulties and conflicts, but this mission is worth the sacrifices. We must choose our battles carefully. My advice is that you look at your own setting with the eyes of compassion, and that you do not fight over inconsequential things, but you will definitely have to confront the challenges with integrity.

It is imperative that we eliminate any possibility of becoming leaders who worship the idol of fear. We can and must anger the devil and a religion without Jesus, shaking up inertia.

You know it. It is always better to fail in the eyes of men than to fail to accomplish the task for which God has summoned us.

> **WE WILL GO THROUGH DIFFICULTIES AND CONFLICTS, BUT THIS MISSION IS WORTH THE SACRIFICES**

Review history, and you will see that the recipe for a revolution begins with an idea, to which a portion of passion mixed with science is added, seasoned by the sauce of perseverance, so it can please the palates of even those who only like eating the same old things.

This has happened with all the paradigm changes, and the implementation of generational leadership will not be an exception.

In heaven there are great expectations regarding what you will accomplish with your ministry starting today. The angels are almost falling from the clouds in their effort to see the church's next move. Jesus of Nazareth, absolute ruler of the universe, is sitting on his throne, watching to see if the church is going to put its attention on the new generations as the situation demands. Others may think that what's truly important always happens far from where they stand, but heaven knows that your decision to develop a vision of generational leadership is vital.

God's promise remains the same:

> See, I am doing a new thing!
> Now it springs up; do you not perceive it?
> I am making a way in the wilderness
> and streams in the wasteland. (Isaiah 43:19)

Trust in him who loves the new generations more than we do. Regardless of what your role is, God has called you to it. DON'T HESITATE TO RESPOND.

Appendix I

QUESTIONS AND ANSWERS ABOUT IMPLEMENTATION

Visions have no feet. They cannot walk alone, let alone run. Visions must be lifted, carried, and placed in visible, well-lit places to allow others to see them and desire to carry them too.

We are the ones who will do the walking, and who will enable the vision to advance too. For that reason, it is important to bring the practical aspect of this book even further by sharing some implementation ideas, and answering questions that I anticipate will arise when trying to bring this vision to reality.

It would be a shame to read this book and think that it contains good ideas, and then do nothing about it. In a very practical sense, ideas, concepts and philosophies do nothing. The leaders are the ones who execute the ideas and enable the philosophies to materialize, and it is incredibly disappointing when good ideas do not see the light because some of us are good at theory, but weak in terms of putting into practice the action plan.

The first question we must answer is …

WHERE DO WE START?

It is very likely that your local church is already practicing some of the things we proposed in this book. I do not think that those of us who speak of generational discipleship are reinventing the wheel. We are simply proposing a better arrangement of musical notes that all of us already know.

Those who are experts in music can explain better than I can that by arranging the same notes in different ways, one can produce different harmonies and musical pieces, and the point here is to determine how we can produce the best harmony with the same notes we already have, before we begin to add some new ones.

The process of materializing the vision of generational leadership in the real world of your congregation should begin in prayer and by sharing the questions that brought about this research with other key people in your congregation.

If you are the pastor, you are at an advantage, because it will be easier for you to change the architecture or the order of your church's procedures. If you are a youth leader or the one in charge of the children's ministry, begin by making sure that your pastor also reads this book.

In fact, a good principle to start implementing what we describe here is for the largest number of key people who form part of the leadership of your congregation to read this material at the same time. This exercise will synchronize the ideas and will help you propose a clearer and more precise work plan to implement the necessary changes.

The second question is ...

WHEN DO WE START?

And the answer is NOT as soon as possible. As we talked about in the chapter on the strategic plan, changes must be made with elegance and the most important changes must be planned as part of a process.

When, as a result of my neuroscience research, I announced to our work team that we were going to change the name of our ministry from Youth Specialties to Specialties 6-25, because of the formal education window that covers ages 6 to 25, we planned a transition. The plan began with months of preparation, during which both names and brands coexisted, and we set a date to officially launch the new name of the ministry, explain the change in a press conference, and make the announcement. We looked for the ideal occasion, and decided to do it with a special first event of dialogue with pastors, which we called the Hispanic Generational Leadership Forum. We wanted to host it in a special place, and by the grace of God we were able to do it at none other than Princeton University.

While we were preparing the launch event, we also worked on our new web page, which we presented on the day of the announcement, but until then we continued to support the service of the previous website, which only disappeared on that day.

I do not share this because I am proposing any name changes or a special event at an academic institution, but because first, I believe that the changes must be planned through transitions, and second, we must look for the ideal occasions to start, which in the case of a local congregation may be when people return from summer vacation, or at the beginning of the school year, or on January of the following year.

Louis Pasteur, the scientist to whom we owe the process of pasteurization, said it very well: "Opportunity favors only the prepared mind." When we prepare a transition plan with enough time, and we begin when we are ready, we'll be better able to take advantage of the opportunities.

HOW DO WE DIVIDE THE AGE GROUPS?

In most Hispanic churches in the U.S. as well as in Latin America, we have on one side the children's ministry and on another side the youth ministry, which does not differentiate between preadolescents, adolescents, youth or "young" dinosaurs. And in most American churches it is standard to follow the school pattern of Elementary, middle and high school but too many churches lack a comprehensive ministry for college age kids.

In this book we explained the science behind drawing the line at 25 years of age, not after as in most Hispanic Churches and not before as in most English-speaking churches.

As far as separating the preadolescents from the children's ministry or from the adolescent ministry, depending on how it's done now in your congregation, this is the stage in which we have the most gray area, because although in the book I talk about ages 11 and 12, here the differences between girls and boys are very noticeable. In girls it is actually between ages 10 and 12, and in boys it is between 11 and 13. I say this because although I believe that each church should establish clear ages to facilitate the transitions from one ministry to another, it is not problematic if some decide to do so after age 10 and others after age 11. In different countries the school stages change differently, and that could be a good parameter for of how we do it.

What's important is to reach the ideal of having each phase well defined, so that there is no gray area in determining when a student must move from one group to the next. These gray areas usually generate doubts and competition between ministries, so it is better, in order to avoid conflict, to have a clearly defined division effective when the school year ends, as sports clubs do with changes in age categories.

WHAT DO WE DO WITH THOSE OVER AGE 26?

What generational leadership proposes is not to discard them, but to graduate them to embrace their adulthood. Of course, no mold is perfect for everyone, and the church will have to address with intelligence how to continue to pastor those who remain single after age 26. One possibility is to involve them in the generational ministry, no longer as consumers but as leaders and mentors (although we must also ensure that they have space for relationships with those their own age).

WHAT IF WE ARE A SMALL CHURCH?

The vision of generational discipleship does not directly concern itself with the size of a church but rather with the proper pastoring of the new generations that we have in our charge.

If the fear is that there are too few at each stage to be able to have separate ministries, it is not necessary to divide them into different meetings. We can separate them during the same meeting. The preadolescent and youth ministries can be together during worship and games, but we can separate them into small groups to discuss the theme of the meeting according to their own needs, placing them in different corners of the same room. In this way we will optimize the resources we have available and generate cohesive spaces to facilitate the spiritual formation of each of them according to their level of maturity.

The good news is that when new generations feel well contained, they become contagious, so by doing this you will have a better chance of multiplying your ministry.

HOW DO WE UNDERTAKE THE BEST TRANSITIONS?

The best transitions are handled with welcomings and graduations. When a student must move from one ministry to another, it should not be something that goes unnoticed. There must be a farewell at the end of the year and a welcoming when the next cycle of meetings begins.

With this I also infer that it is a missed opportunity not to have vacations from meetings and programs. Remember that God does not attend the church only on weekends, and alternating cycles of meetings does not offend a God who is more concerned about us and what we do every day than whether some weeks a year we may not have a meeting.

HOW DO WE RECRUIT AND ORGANIZE THE BEST TEAM?

In the chapters of this book we repeated several times that we must add adults to the ministry to the new generations, and we also highlighted the need to expose the new generations to marriage models.

We also talked about adding models from the next level of maturity, and that is why we must think about how to add some preadolescents as volunteers in the children's ministry, some adolescents in the ministry with the preadolescents and youth in the adolescent ministry.

Of course, not everyone can be a leader, but we can be sure that the more leaders we have, the better pastored our new generations will be.

Make open calls and set up job interviews to choose your leaders. Evaluate not only their skills but their motivations. Why does someone want to be in that ministry? Set timetables. Accepting a position should not be for an indefinite period of time. If we talk about those in charge of specific stages, then the commitment should be for at least three years, in order to have longevity and consistency in the ministries. But in the case of servants and volunteers who will help with more general tasks, the commitment can be set for one year, and renewed annually if necessary.

My practical observation of the ideal teams is that this architecture of generational leadership can give the responsibility of children and youth leadership to one married couple who oversees all generational work, and this couple will recruit leaders for the different stages.

And let's talk straight... dear pastor, this can also be an advantage for the church budget. Having a couple as generational pastors who will link the teams of the four stages, from childhood to youth, is cheaper than trying to have caretakers of children and youth pastors in your congregation. Of course, as the ministry grows and if you have the possibility of doing so, you may eventually have a full staff, under the generational pastors.

WHAT IS NEUROSCIENCE?

This may not be a question about practical implementation, but when we start talking about these changes, some adults may be interested in investigating exactly what we are talking about, and that is why I answer that neuroscience is the interdisciplinary study of the nervous system, and its main goal is the understanding of the brain in relation to behavior.

The enthusiasm about this field arises from the attempt to discover and explain the organ that defines a being as an individual, controlling his actions, generating his emotions and editing his memories. Today, thanks to technology, neuronal movements can be seen or read in real time, which allows us to learn how the brain behaves under different stimuli and actions.

HOW DO WE INVOLVE PARENTS?

Call a special meeting for parents, and start by explaining what the vision of generational leadership is all about. (You can use the video of the basic diagram of Generational Leadership that can be downloaded at the Premium Zone of e625.com.)

In that first meeting, enable them to understand and value the strategic alliance that you will be able to build together for the spiritual formation of the new generations. Explain to them the plan of action and when you'll start the concrete changes in the ministry, but assure them that outside of any structure, this will start with a spiritual partnership.

Ask parents how you can support them in the spiritual development of their children. The mere fact that you ask them that question will lead them to reflection.

According to their criteria, what is a child's greatest need, and what can you do to help them fill that need? How can you pray for their families? Working with the new generations is much more effective when church leaders and parents are praying for the same needs.

Be intentional in adding the church as a resource for parents, and they will be much more open to support the needs of the congregation's programs and help out with their time and resources when needed.

When everything starts to be implemented, create at least once-a-year activities where children and their parents can serve together. When children serve together with their parents, the impact is threefold in their lives because serving to them is an adventure, their parents also serve, and they do it together, so we all win.

Appendix II

GENERATIONAL LEADERSHIP AND THEOLOGY

There are truths and doctrines that must be internalized by each member of the church, and there is no better occasion for that to happen than during the maturation process that takes place from childhood to youth.

It saddens me when in some places I hear that people believe that theology is boring and without any practical relevance. It absolutely is not. Theology conditions the Christian experience. What we believe about God and our faith directly affects both the way we hear his voice and whether we embrace or reject his proposals. That's why all Christians should place importance on personally embracing biblical theology.

Beyond contemporary programs, friendships, pedagogical techniques, and leadership tactics, there are things that cannot be neglected, and those are the basic doctrines of our faith.

The well-known Peruvian thinker and writer Samuel Escobar wrote many years ago that "evangelical churches are first of all a theological reality. They conceive themselves as expressions of God's people on earth and are defined according to biblical terms as the body of Christ, family of God, royal priesthood, acquired people".[1]

---

1   Escobar 1977:44

Sometimes it scares me to see some sectors of the church that know more Christian songs than fundamental Bible texts. That is part of the challenge and opportunity presented to us by generational leadership. Our ministries become more vibrant spiritually when teachers and students learn together the word of God and build a disciplined theological structure that we can share with confidence.

Who is God? What are his intentions? These are two basic questions that give rise to all Judeo-Christian theology and also to the biblical foundations of generational ministry.

Among the many things that the Bible highlights about who God is, perhaps the most concise is the clearest: God is love (1 John 4:8). That love, as far as we are concerned, reached its climax in the sacrifice of Christ on the cross (John 3:16). Why did Christ die? Because he wants to save us from the wages of sin, which is death (Romans 6:23; 2 Peter 3:9). It may seem unnecessary to mention these principles as an appendix to this book, but the truth is that in times when the production of shows is one of the most profitable industries on the planet and leaders begin to increasingly feel the pressure of numerical multiplication, it is necessary to insist on the core of the gospel.

Every ministry to children, preadolescents, adolescents and young people should clearly state the answers to those first two questions, but we cannot just stay there.

THE IMPORTANT ISSUES

The following important issues should be reviewed over and over again in our ministries, in order to build a well-founded biblical theology.

1. GOD

Who does he say he is? The first thing that God reveals in his Scriptures is himself. Personal pronouns, anthropomorphisms and his character as revealed in his dealings with human beings give us a glimpse of God himself, expressed in the three persons of the Trinity. It is vital to hear what God has to say about himself, and that is why the attributes of each person in the Trinity must constitute fundamental theological foundations of our ministries. An interesting idea to follow as a teaching program is the names of God and their meanings.

2. CHRIST

The person of Christ is the central axis of our faith, and must be the doctrinal framework through which all other truths are interpreted. As I explained in the chapter about cultural intelligence, Jesus is the language of God. He is the model, compass and map of Christian behavior, and the new generations must clearly learn that Jesus is inescapable, even beyond our religious experiences. Jesus is in the calendar, in the genesis of the history of Europe, in the confluence of Semitic religions, in the caravels that crossed the Atlantic to discover the New World, in the pilgrims who founded North America and in the Jesuits who accompanied gold prospectors to the jungles of South America. Jesus continues to appear in political speeches and in those of artists who receive an Oscar or a Grammy for their movies or songs. His person is in the name of countries and dozens of cities. Jesus is a movie and a Broadway play. He is song, industry, literature and painting. He is still in a cup of milk that an orphan receives, in the hand that touches a leper in Calcutta, and in the person who visits an old man without family at a public hospital. And as if all this were not enough, our beliefs about his deity and his humanity determine not just our ethics on earth, but also our eternal destiny.

3. SCRIPTURES

The Bible is a letter of invitation to know God and his will. It says, "Faith comes from hearing the message, and the message is heard through the word about Christ" (Romans 10:17). Something miraculous happens when communicating the Scriptures under the anointing of the Holy Spirit.

The importance of the Bible must be recognized and taught to each generation, and one of the best ways to do it with a generation that prefers relationships and experiment is to focus on the use of stories. It is very likely that when Jesus chose to communicate with parables, he did so to show his truths as timeless, and to make them relevant to different cultures in different eras. Our mission as generational leaders is to show that the Scriptures are attractive and relevant to everyday life.

4. HUMANITY

A healthy biblical anthropology should be another one of the blocks on which we support our ministries. Many times Christians are so focused on what people should be doing that we pay very little attention to what they are actually doing and why they say they do it. "Good anthropologists try to discover what's already there before theorizing about what people should do."[2] I do not say that we should become "anthropologists" in every sense of the word, but we can learn to define, based on the Bible and what we see in our communities, the condition of human beings and their needs.

This type of anthropology is a good foundation, yet the necessary research can become very exciting for a new generations group, if creative methods of collecting information are established and if the new generations are allowed to creatively think about it. What has God already said about the condition of man and woman? This is a very important question in the midst of a pop Christian society where it seems that we just want to flatter customers by avoiding moral standards.

5. SIN

Each point is derived from the previous one, and in this case sin is part of the answer to the last question. Based on the ideas of the New

2   (Kraft 1996:4).

Age movement that became popular with cultural elites several years ago, or the aforementioned individualism and relativism prevailing since postmodernism, a clear definition of sin must be present. On many occasions, and I must say in many congregations, children, and especially adolescents, are told a lot about specific sins, but little about "sin" as a theological reality. Also, when talking about the sins to which the new generations are exposed, care must be taken to be biblical and not to label as sins things that are simply not attractive to our own eyes and customs. Another requirement is not to condemn without offering a way out. We must always be sensitive to the condition in which people find themselves, and focus on restoration, even as we make it clear that restoration comes through repentance. That is why we must call evil what it is, without shortcuts.

6. REDEMPTION

How to get free from the power of sin? Our new identity in Christ must be clearly explained. What is the scope of salvation? What are its immediate and mediate consequences? I have encountered too many children of believers born into the church who reach adolescence without a clear idea about salvation. I like the description of evangelism made by Professor Charles Van Engen in his book *Mission on the Way*. In it, this mission theology professor says that "evangelization must be faith-particularist, culturally-pluralist and ecclesiologically-inclusive."[3] The statement "Jesus Christ is Lord" has no competition, and that is why our evangelism does not resemble the message of any other religion. We are different, unique. At the same time, there are many ways and forms to enjoy the consequences of redemption and to express that faith. That is why we must be culturally pluralistic.

Finally, an interest in the growth of the kingdom of God on earth should permeate our evangelical practice, and that is why we must always remember that local churches exist to keep adding people to the church of Christ.

---

3   (Van Engen 1996:183-187)

7. FAITH COMMUNITY

What is the church? What is it for? What should it produce? John Stott also said, "The entire Bible is rich in evidence of God's missionary purpose,"[4] and so in this book we analyzed the purposes of the ministry in detail. Without knowing the true nature of the church it is impossible to enjoy it and build it in accordance with its divine design. A ministry to the new generations that does not have a solid ecclesiastical foundation will lack transcendent goals and will cultivate a disoriented generation that will end up producing disoriented churches.

8. HOLY SPIRIT

Who is the Holy Spirit? What is his role? How do we live in the Spirit? It is impossible to live the Christian life without the power of the Holy Spirit. The fruit of the Spirit (Galatians 5:22–25) is the sign of true Christianity, and without his guidance and help it is impossible to fulfill God's purposes for the church. Without a solid doctrine regarding the Holy Spirit, the church falters between, in one extreme, understanding the Spirit as some mystical energy that is present only in some who have spectacular gifts, and, at the other extreme, seeing him as a seal without any practical connotations.

9. MISSION

In Ephesians 2:10 the apostle Paul makes it clear that we are God's engineering, designed for good works. Every Christian has a call that's like a coin with two faces: to be more like Jesus (Romans 8:29; Ephesians 4:13), and to be a blessing to others (1 Peter 2:9; Ephesians 1:12–14). These are two truths that go hand in hand. The new generations need to learn and embrace the fact that this call is experienced in different ways and manifests itself in different ways, but it's for all of us who recognize Jesus as our Savior and our Lord.

---

4   (Stott 1979:10)

In Paul's words: "And whatever you do, whether in word or deed, do it all in the name of the Lord Jesus, giving thanks to God the Father through him" (Colossians 3:17).

Finally, these nine topics in this appendix cannot become only theoretical and impractical knowledge. Two types of applications must accompany them.

A. **Personal applications:** What does each of these topics mean for the lives of leaders (what does it mean for you) and for the lives of new generations?

B. **Ministerial applications:** How is each of these points embodied in the life of the ministry of which we are a part?

The personal theology of those of us who teach has a strong effect on those who learn from us, since in everything we teach and in everything we do we are communicating our theology. This is why establishing clear convictions on these nine major issues will prevent us from adding more confusion to a generation that already receives too many conflicting messages.

The captains of ancient ships used to tie the compasses to their bodies when they were in the middle of a storm. Likewise, generational leaders must tie the Bible to our lives to discern at every moment the path of God's will in order to guide this generation to a safe harbor.

BIBLIOGRAPHY

Aamodt, Sandra, and Sam Wang
2011   *Welcome to Your Child's Brain (Bienvenido al cerebro de tu hijo)*. New York, NY: MJF Books.

Anderson, Neil, and Rich Miller
1997   *Leading Teenagers to Freedom in Christ (Guiando adolescentes a la libertad en Cristo)*. Ventura, CA: Regal Books.

Anthony, Michael J.
2006   *Perspectives on Children's Spiritual Formation (Perspectivas en la formación espiritual de los niños)*. Nashville, TN: B&N Publishing Group.

Arthur, Chris (Ed.)
1993   *Religion and the Media (La Religión y los Medios)*. Cardiff, Wales: University of Wales Press.

Barchetta, Carmen
1994   *Adolescentes* 1994. En Quehacer Femenino 128:5–6.

Barna, George
1995   *Generation Next (La próxima generación)*. Ventura, CA: Regal Books.

1997   *Leaders on Leadership (Líderes sobre liderazgo)*. Ventura, CA: Regal Books.

2001   *Real Teens (Adolescentes reales)*. Ventura, CA: Regal Books – Youth Specialties.

Bauer, Susan Wise, and Jessie Wise
2009   *The Well-Trained Mind (La mente bien entrenada)*. New York, NY: W. W. Norton & Company, Inc.

Berzonsky, Michael D.
1981   *Adolescent Development (Desarrollo Adolescente).* New York, NY: Macmillan Publishing Co., Inc.

Blake, R. R. and Mouton, J. S.
1964   *The Managerial Grid (La cuadrícula administrativa).* Houston, TX: Gulf.

Boshers, Bo
1997   *Student Ministry for the 21st Century (Ministerio estudiantil para el siglo veintiuno).* Grand Rapids, MI: Zondervan Publishing House.

Brister, C. W.
1988   *El cuidado pastoral en la Iglesia (Pastoral care in the Church).* El Paso, TX: Casa Bautista de Publicaciones.

Cimo, Pat and Markins, Matt
2016   *Leading KidMin (Liderando el ministerio de niños).* Chicago, IL: Moody Publishers.

Clark, Chap
1997   *The Youth Worker's Handbook to Family Ministry (Manual del Ministerio Familiar para trabajadores juveniles).* El Cajón, CA: Youth Specialties.

Clinton, J. Robert
1986   *Leadership Emergence Patterns (Patrones del liderazgo emergente).* Altadena, CA: Barnabas Resources.

Daniel J. Siegel, M.D.
2015   *Brainstorm: The Power and Purpose of the Teenage Brain (Lluvia de ideas: el poder y el propósito del cerebro adolescente).* New York, NY: Jeremy P. Tarcher/Penguin.

Dean, Kenda Creasy, Chap Clark, and Dave Rahn

2001   *Starting Right (Empezando bien)*. El Cajon, CA: Youth Specialties.

Deiros, Pablo A.

1997   *Diccionario Hispanoamericano de la Misión (Hispano-American Dictionary of the Mission)* . Miami, FL: Comibam Internacional, Editorial Unilit.

De Pree, Max

2001   *Called to Serve: Creating and Nurturing the Effective Volunteer Board (Llamados para servir: creando y nutriendo un grupo efectivo de voluntarios)*. Grand Rapids, MI: Wm B. Eerdmans Publishing Co.

Dettoni, John M.

1993   *Introduction to Youth Ministry (Introducción al ministerio juvenil)*. Grand Rapids, MI: Zondervan Publishing House.

1997   *Philosophy and Models of Youth Ministry (Filosofía y modelos de ministerio juvenil)*. CF 540, class material. Pasadena, CA: Fuller Theological Seminary, School of World Mission.

Devries, Raúl A. and Alicia Pallone de Devries

1995   *Adolescencia, desafío para padres (Adolescence, challenge for parents)*. Buenos Aires: Paidos.

Diaz, April L.

2013   *Redefining the Role of the Youth Worker (Redefiniendo el rol del líder juvenil)*. The Youth Cartel.

Dunn, Richard R.

1997   *A Theological Framework for Doing Youth Ministry (Un marco teológico para hacer ministerio juvenil). In Reaching a Generation for Christ (Alcanzando una generación para*

Cristo). Richard R. Dunn and Mark H. Senter, eds. Chicago, IL: Moody Press.

Escobar, Samuel
1977   *Irrupción juvenil (Juvenile eruption)*. Miami, FL: Editorial Caribe. Fiedler, F. E.

1967   *A Theory of Leadership Effectiveness (Una teoría de la efectividad del liderazgo)*. New York, NY: McGraw-Hill.

Fields, Doug
2000   *Ministerio de Jóvenes con Propósito (Purpose Youth Ministry)*. Miami, FL: Vida/Especialidades Juveniles.

2002   *Your First Two Years in Youth Ministry (Tus primeros dos años en el ministerio juvenil)*. El Cajon, CA: Youth Specialties.

Freberg, Laura A.
2015   *Discovering Behavioral Neuroscience (Descubriendo la neurociencia de la conducta)*. MA: Wadsworth Publishing.

Gallagher, Roswell J.
1983   *"Impacto que causan los familiares, maestros y compañeros sobre los adolescentes." En Medicina de la Adolescencia ("Impact that family members, teachers and classmates have on adolescents." In Adolescent Medicine)*. Jerome T. Y. Shen, ed. Pp. 20–27. México D. F.: Editorial El Manual Moderno S. A.

Hersey, Paul, Kenneth Blanchard, and Dewy E. Johnson
1996   *Management of Organizational Behavior (Administración del comportamiento organizacional)*. Upper Saddle River, NJ: Prentice Hall.

Jeeves, Malcom, and Warren S. Brown
2009   *Neurociencia, psicología y religión (Neuroscience, psychology and religion)*. Navarra, España: Editorial Verbo Divino.

Jensen, Frances E., and Amy Ellis Nutt
2015   *The Teenage Brain (El cerebro adolescente).* New York, NY: Harper Collins Publishers.

Joiner, Reggie
2009   *Think Orange (Piensa en naraja).* GA: Orange Books.

Joiner, Reggie, and Kristen Ivy
2015   *It's Just a Phase, So Don't Miss It (Es solo una fase, así que no te la pierdas).* GA. Orange Books.

Kageler, Len
2008   *The Youth Ministry Survival Guide: How to Thrive and Last for the Long Haul (La guía de supervivencia del ministerio juvenil: cómo desarrollarse y mantenerse a largo plazo).* Grand Rapids, MI: Zondervan.

Keller, Thimoty
2012   *Every Good Enderavor (Cada buen esfuerzo).* New York, NY: Dutton.

Kinnaman, David
2016   *You Lost Me (Me perdieron).* Grand Rapids, MI: Baker Books.

Kolb, David A.
2015   *Experiential Learning: Experience as the Source of Learning and Development (Aprendizaje experimental: La experiencia como Fuente de aprendizaje y desarrollo).* NJ: Pearson Education.

Konterlink, Irene, and Claudia Jacinto
1996   *Adolescencia, pobreza, educación y trabajo (Adolescence, poverty, education and work).* Buenos Aires, Argentina: Losada y UNICEF.

Kraft, Charles
1996   *Anthropology for Christian Witness (Antropología para el testimonio cristiano).* Maryknoll, NY: Orbis Books.

Livermore, David A.
2009   *Cultural Intelligence (Inteligencia Cultural).* Grand Rapids, MI: Baker Academic.

Lovaglia, Daniel M.
2016   Relational Children's Ministry (Ministerio de niños relacional). Grand Rapids, MI: Zondervan.

Lyotard, Jean-Francois
1995   *La condición postmoderna (The postmodern condition).* Buenos Aires, Argentina: Editorial Rei.

Mardones, José María
1991   *Capitalismo y religión (Capitalism and religion).* Bilbao, Spain: Editorial Sal Terrae.

Maxwell, John C.
1996   Desarrolle el líder que está en usted (Develop the leader inside you). Nashville, TN: Editorial Caribe.

2001   *Las 17 leyes incuestionables del trabajo en equipo (The 17 unquestionable laws of teamwork).* Nashville, TN: Editorial Caribe- Betania.

Maxwell, John C., and Les Parrott.
2005   *25 Ways to Win People: How to Make Others Feel Like a Million Bucks (25 maneras de ganarse a la gente: cómo hacer que el otro se sienta como si valiera un millón de dólares).* Nashville, TN: Thomas Nelson, Inc.

McLaren, Brian D.
2000   *The Church on the Other Side (La iglesia del otro lado).* Grand Rapids, MI: Zondervan.

Merton Strommen, Karen E. Jones, and Dave Rahn
2001   *Youth Ministry that Transforms (Ministerio juvenil que transforma).* El Cajon, CA: Youth Specialties.

Mueller, Walt
1994   *Understanding Today's Youth Culture (Entendiendo la cultura juvenil de hoy).* Wheaton, IL: Tyndale House Publishers.

Myers Blair, Glenn, and R. Stewart Jones
1984   *Cómo es el adolescente y cómo educarlo (How is the adolescent and how to educate him).* Buenos Aires, Argentina: Editorial Paidos.

Nelsen, Jane, Lynn Lott, and H. Stephen Glenn.
2007   *Positive Discipline A–Z: 1001 Solutions to Everyday Parenting Problems (Disciplina positiva de la A a la Z: 1001 soluciones para los problemas cotidianos de la paternidad).* New York, NY: Three Rivers Press.

Nietzsche, Friedrich
1988   *El Crepúsculo de los Ídolos (The Twilight of the Idols).* Buenos Aires, Argentina: Editorial Petrel.

Obiols, Guillermo A., and Silvia Di Segni de Obiols
1996   *Adolescencia, posmodernidad y escuela secundaria (Adolescence, postmodernity and high school).* Buenos Aires, Argentina: Editorial Kapeluz.

Oestreicher, Mark
2008   *Youth Ministry 3.0 (Ministerio de Jóvenes 3.0).* Grand Rapids, MI: Zondervan.

2012   *A Parent's Guide to Understanding Teenage Brains (Guía para padres para entender el cerebro adolescente)*. CO: Group Publishing.

Ortíz, Felix
2008   *Raíces: Pastoral juvenil en profundidad (Roots: Youth ministry in depth)*. Miami, FL: Especialidades Juveniles.

2017   *Cada joven necesita un mentor (Every young person needs a mentor)*. Dallas, TX. E625.com.

Pérez, Roberto
1994   *Adolescencia, desafío de ser persona ("Adolescence, challenge of being a person)*. Unpublished anthropological essay.

Philips, Tom
1997   *Building a Team to Get the Job Done (Edificando un equipo para lograr hacer el trabajo)*. In *Leaders on Leadership (Líderes sobre liderazgo)*. George Barna, ed. Ventura, CA: Regal Books.

Piaget, Jean, Anna Freud, and J. Osterreich
1977   *El desarrollo del adolescente (Adolescent development)*. Buenos Aires, Argentina: Editorial Paidos.

Powell, Kara, and Chap Clark
2011   *Sticky Faith (Una fe pegajosa)*. Grand Rapids, MI: Zondervan.

Powell, Kara, Jake Mulde, and Brad Griffin.
2016   *Growing Young: Six Essential Strategies to Help Young People Discover and Love Your Church (Haciéndose jóven: seis estrategias esenciales para ayudar a los jóvenes a descubrir y amar tu iglesia)*. Grand Rapids, MI: Baker Books.

Rich, Dorothy

2008 *Megaskills: Building Our Children's Character and Achievement for School and Life (Mega habilidades. Construyendo el carácter y la habilidad de los niños para la escuela y la vida)*. IL: Sourcebooks Inc.

Schipani, Daniel S.

1993 *Teología del ministerio educativo (Theology of the educational ministry)*. Buenos Aires, Argentina: Nueva Creación.

Schteingart, Mario

1964 *La adolescencia normal y sus trastornos endócrinos (Theology of the educational ministry)*. Buenos Aires, Argentina: Héctor Macchi Ediciones.

Senter, Mark, III

1992 *The Coming Revolution in Youth Ministry (La revolución que viene en el ministerio juvenil)*. Wheaton, IL: Víctor Books.

Shaffer, David R.

1989 *Developmental Psychology, Childhood and Adolescence (Psicología del desarrollo, niñez y adolescencia)*. Second edition. Pacific Grove, CA: Brooks-Cole Publishing Company.

Souza, David A.

2016 *How the Brain Learns (Cómo aprende el cerebro)*. CA: Sage Publications.

Stone L. J., and J. Church

1968 *El adolescente de 13 a 20 años (The teenager from 13 to 20 years old)*. Buenos Aires, Argentina: Editorial Paidos.

Stott, John

1974 *Creer es también pensar (Believing is also thinking)*. Buenos Aires, Argentina: Ediciones Certeza.

1979   *The Living God Is a Missionary God (El Dios vivo es un Dios misionero). In You Can Tell the World (Puedes decírselo al mundo)*, James E. Berney, ed. Pp. 10–18. Downers Grove, IL: InterVarsity Press.

Sweet, Leonard L.
1998   *Aquachurch (Iglesia acuática)*. Loveland, CO: Group Publishing.

Tolbert, La Verne
2004   *Enseñemos como Jesús (Let's teach like Jesus)*. Miami, FL: Editorial Vida.

Tracy, Brian
2015   *Delegación y supervisión (Delegation and supervision)*. Nashville, TN: Grupo Nelson.

Van Engen, Charles
1996   *Mission on the Way (Misión en el camino)*. Grand Rapids, MI: Baker Books.

Walton, Dr. David
2012   *Emotional Intelligence (Inteligencia emocional)*. New York, NY: MJF Books.

Warren, Rick
1995   *Una Iglesia con Propósito (The porpuse driven church)*. Miami, FL: Editorial Vida.

Webb, Keith
2012   *Coach Model (El modelo coach)*. Miami, FL: Active Results, LLC.

Yarhouse, Mark A.
2013   *Understanding Sexual Identity (Entendiendo la identidad sexual)*. Grand Rapids, MI: Zondervan.

SOME QUESTIONS TO ANSWER:

WHO IS BEHIND THIS BOOK?

E625 is a team of pastors and servants from different countries, different denominations, different sizes and church styles who love Christ and the new generations.

e625.com

WHAT IS E625.COM ABOUT?

Our passion is to help families and churches to find good materials and resources for the discipleship of new generations and that is why our website serves parents, pastors, teachers, and leaders 365 days a year through **www.e625.com** with free resources.

zona de contenido
PREMIUM

WHAT IS THE PREMIUM SERVICE?

In addition to free reflections and short materials, we have a service of lessons, series, research, online books, and audiovisual resources to facilitate your task. Your church can access them with a monthly subscription that allows all the leaders of a local church to share them as a team and make the necessary copies that they find pertinent to the different activities of the congregation or its families.

CAN I EQUIP MYSELF WITH YOU?

It would be a privilege to help you and with that objective, you can choose seminars at **www.e625.com** and academic courses at **www.institutoE625.com**.

Sign up for e625.com updates right now depending on your work arena: Pastors - Children - Preadolescents - Adolescents - College ministry.

LET'S LEARN TOGETHER!

e625.com

 /e625COM

Magazine

Books

Chat

Downloads
Subscription

Store

Events

Seminars

INSTITUTO
e6
25

Online Education
www.InstitutoE625.com

e625.com